D0069185

In Our Lady's Shadow

The Spirituality of Praying for Priests

Mary Kloska

En Route Books & Media, LLC
St. Louis, MO

⊕ENROUTE
Make the time

En Route Books and Media, LLC

5705 Rhodes Avenue

St. Louis, MO 63109

Cover credit: Dr. Sebastian Mahfood, OP

Copyright © 2021 Mary Kloska

All rights reserved.

Contact us at contactus@enroutebooksandmedia.com

Library of Congress Control Number: 2021934578

ISBN-13: 978-1-952464-66-9 and 978-1-952464-68-3

No part of this book may be reproduced, stored in a retrieval system, or transmitted in any form, or by any means, electronic, mechanical, photocopying, or otherwise, without the prior written permission of the authors.

This book is consecrated to my Sweet Jesus,
The Victim, the Altar and the Eternal High Priest.
And to His Mother –the Mother of all Priests –who lived as
His Helpmate in His Priestly Work.

This book is also written as a gift to all of the priests who have
provided me with the sacraments in my lifetime, those who
generously spent hours giving me spiritual direction, those who
extended brotherly friendship to me and those whose
priesthoods have been especially entrusted to my life of prayer
and sacrifice.

Contents

Introduction

The word 'compassion' means 'to suffer with'—in some ways it means 'you're suffering in my heart.' How could such a thing be possible? St. Thomas Aquinas speaks on spiritual friendship explaining how after a while two people who love each other deeply and share a friendship experience a compenetration of hearts—where it almost seems like they share one heart in two bodies. If such a union of love can be reached simply through human friendship, how much more was such a union of love reached by Our Lady and Jesus? In this way, Mary lived the essence of 'Com-passion' with Jesus in the ultimate way.

In Eden when Adam was presented with Eve—formed by God from his side while he slept in the Garden—he exclaimed, 'This one at last is bone of my bones and flesh of my flesh!' In a reversal of roles, in the little kitchen garden of Nazareth while Our Lady prayed Her noonday prayer, an angel came to Her and asked Her to be the Mother of God. When She said, 'Yes—Fiat!' to the angel, the Holy Spirit overshadowed Her and formed from Her Heart the little Body of Our Lord—the Second Person of the Trinity Incarnate. Here She exclaimed, 'This one at last is bone of my bones and flesh of my flesh!' What union this Mother and Child had—as every atom of human DNA in Jesus' body came from His Mother. And still their union was even deeper, as Our Lady's soul was immaculate and totally consumed with His Divine Love. Yet, what a tragic destiny this little Mother had laid before Her that sunny afternoon as She prayed at home. Her Heart that was so intertwined with the Heart of Her Little Savior formed within Her womb would be called to a destiny as grave as His. He was a Child—and yet He would be the Victim, the Altar, the Eternal High Priest that would consummate the ultimate sacrifice that redeemed all of humanity. Every fingerprint of suffering that He would endure in His earthly life She would endure united one with Him as both His Mother and His Helpmate under the Cross.

We see the mystery of Christ imprinting His Love upon His chosen souls early on in the Church as we are told the story of St. Veronica on the Way of the Cross. An ordinary woman who sees the suffering Lord dragging His Cross painstakingly down the street is moved by the Holy Spirit to run to Him and wipe His face in a cloth to give Him a little relief. And yet it is He who leaves His image imprinted upon Her veil—His face radiant in Crucified Majesty— clearly to be seen for centuries to come. And still greater, even more than leaving His Face imprinted upon a piece of cloth, He left His Image imprinted upon the heart of sweet

Veronica. She carried His suffering look within the confines of her heart all the days of her life.

In a similar way, we see the Lord imprinting His Holy Passion upon the hearts of His saints throughout the history of the Church. For example, in 1294 St. Clare of Montefalco entered a coma-like state of ecstasy and survived only through the diligent care of her fellow nuns. When she woke, she testified that she had met Christ in the guise of a pilgrim carrying the cross. He informed Clare that her heart proved strong enough in faith for him to "rest" his burden there. Thereafter, Clare described having chronic pain in her chest until her death. When Clare died, the sisters of her monastery performed an unofficial autopsy on her heart and discovered a crucifix made of flesh. The instruments of the passion, including a small scourge and three nails made of nerve fiber, were removed from the same heart three days after the discovery of the fleshly crucifix. After significant controversy and an official inquisition immediately following Clare's death, the local bishop determined that the relics were authentic.

In a different way, the Lord imprinted His suffering upon St. Gemma Gilgani. On June 8, 1899, St. Gemma was told in prayer to prepare for a great grace. Later that day she recalls...

"At that moment Jesus appeared with all His wounds open, but blood no longer came out of

those wounds. Rather, flames of fire issued forth from them and in an instant these flames came to touch my hands, my feet, and my heart. I felt as if I would die. I fell to the floor, but my Mother supported me, keeping me covered in her mantle. I had to remain several hours in that position. Finally, she kissed me on my forehead, and all vanished, and I found myself kneeling on the floor. But I still felt an intense pain in my hands, feet, and heart. I arose to go to bed, and I then noticed that blood was flowing from those parts where I felt pain. I covered them as well as I could, and then with the help of my angel, I was able to go to bed. These sufferings and pains, although they afflicted me, filled me with perfect peace. The next morning, I was able to go to Communion only with great difficulty, and I put on a pair of gloves in order to hide my hands. I could hardly stand on my feet, and I thought I would die at any minute. The sufferings continued until 3pm on Friday afternoon, the solemnity of the Sacred Heart of Jesus."

As we strive in this book to enter the spirituality of praying for priests with the spirit of Our Lady, we must see at the onset that more than praying for the man-priest, we are accompanying Jesus on His Way of Calvary. It is by Jesus' imprinting His suffering upon our hearts as we gaze upon Him, contemplating His gift, His wounds, His crucified Love, that we will in turn become helpmates of His suffering as Our Lady was. And then He, in turn, will use our prayer and suffering to apply needed graces to our priest brothers, priest sons, priest fathers—all the ordained men of God entrusted to our prayer.

The work of praying for priests must center on Jesus crucified—by uniting our hearts one with His, the way that Our Lady's Heart was united one with His—otherwise, our work will be merely human and fruitless. In fact, if Jesus' Life, Death, and Resurrection as the Eternal High Priest is not the center of our prayer, then the work of praying for priests could lead a soul into clinging to an ordinary man, and this would be a distraction from God's work of uniting a soul to God. The more we contemplate and love Jesus as the Eternal High Priest—as Our Lady did—the more we will help the souls of priests for whom we intercede. And if we do this work of prayer with Our Lady, like Our Lady (who is the Mother of all priests), then we will be drawn intimately close to Jesus Himself simply through selflessly praying for His priest sons.

I hope and pray that by reading this book your hearts may be imprinted with an image of Christ's Love as tangible as that held by St. Veronica, St. Clare of Montefalco, and St. Gemma Gilagani—even if it is not visible to the eyes. I pray that your hearts will be transformed to conform unto His Sacred Heart as His

Mother's Heart did—standing strong in brave Trust and Surrender on Calvary. May Our Lady, the Helpmate of Jesus the Eternal High Priest, teach us to love as She does, pray as She does, serve as She does—and may this grace bear fruit in holy priestly vocations throughout the entire world.

Fiat. Amen. So be it. +

Chapter 1

Our Lady—the Mother of the Eternal High Priest—Little Jesus Crucified

The Little Mary—Immaculate Conception and Life in the Temple

The beginning of Our Lady's story as the Mother of the Eternal High Priest began in Her own conception. Somehow, mysteriously, the merits of Her Son Jesus on Calvary were applied to Her earlier in time so that She could be conceived without the trace of any sin. The Father desired this so that He would have an immaculate bed—the land of Her Heart—within which to place His Son. Just as an altar, a chalice, a paten—everything used in the Liturgy at Mass—is especially set aside from ordinary use—consecrated for the work of being a pure and holy vessel for the worshiping of God, so, too, Our Lady's Heart was set aside from the very first moments of Her conception as a pure and unspoiled resting place for the Divine. As we contemplate Little Miriam of Nazareth— the little, innocent bed of love where the Father would lay His Son—praying in Her parents' garden, praying in the Temple, inspiring the High Priest by Her simple presence—the Joy of the Eternal Father as He gazed upon the earth—then we have a glimpse of the sort of innocence God is calling us to live if we are called to give our lives to praying for priests.

What were the virtues that the Trinity planted so profoundly in little Mary's Heart that grew under the influence of the Holy Spirit's grace to prepare Her to be the Tabernacle of Her Son, Jesus? St. Louis de Montfort points to 10 principal virtues that Our Lady embodied—and these virtues allowed Her to be the greatest helpmate and intercessor along with Her son, the Eternal High Priest, on Calvary. When Mary is called the 'Mystic Rose,' She is the perfect flower—without thorns—that gives forth the fragrance of holiness and perpetual prayer. The petals of Her flower are each a different virtue, and we should strive in imitation of Our Lady to imitate these virtues, being Her Angelic Sweetness, Ardent Charity, Blind Obedience, Constant Mental Prayer, Divine Purity, Divine Wisdom, Heroic Patience, Lively Faith, Profound Humility, and Universal Mortification.

If we are to pray for priests, we have to strive to be holy as Our Lady was holy. Their priesthoods should become holier because of our prayer—not corrupted by our sinfulness. If one is committed to praying for priests, she must be committed to a life of regular Confession, Adoration where she is washed in the presence of God, striving for virtue throughout her days. The prayers of the innocent are so powerful before the Throne of Heaven—which is why I always encouraged the ministry of children committed to praying for particular priests. I would print out pictures of priests I had met in various missions and entrust them to my nieces and nephews—knowing that their hearts naïve of real sin would be clamorous voices before the Throne of God for these priests' vocations.

And yet, one should not fear her littleness and failings when she trips over herself during the day. God knows every heart. One must strive for holiness—strive for humility—strive for purity—strive for authentic selfless-ness—but when she falls, she must remember what He said in the defense of the sinful woman (Luke 7:44-47)—*Those who are forgiven much, love much."* A spiritual mother and sister to priests must use her faults and failings as tools to grow in humility—as ember to enflame her love for Jesus—as fire to throw her closer to Him—as courage to embolden her to claim His Mercy and to open her to be a greater torrent of His Merciful Love to the priests for whom she is interceding. She must be patient with their weakness because the Lord is patient with her weakness. She must excuse and encourage them because the Lord excuses, forgives, and encourages her. And yet she must never turn away from striving daily towards that ideal…hiding herself in the Heart of Mary so that Her Love, Her virtue, Her Prayer may work from within her.

The Lord hid Mary in the Temple when She was three years old—and while spending Her life among the little virgins singing to God and literally spending their innocent lives in worship of the Almighty—the Holy Spirit continued to knit His graces, gifts and fruits within Our Lady's Heart. Her desire for the Savior—an Eternal Priest Who would save Her people—began as a little spark within Her Heart but grew to a burning flame behind the curtain of the Temple. This desire placed within Her by God only grew to an insatiable, prayerful thirst that eventually called the Almighty to look with mercy on His people and send the Angel Gabriel to bring the good news to His worthy Little Daughter. Mary had already been betrothed to St. Joseph and was preparing for a life united with him in pure love when the Angel came to Her in prayer and said:

Annunciation—Luke 1:26-38

"In the sixth month, the angel Gabriel was sent from God to a town of Galilee called Nazareth, to a virgin betrothed to a man named Joseph, of the house of David, and the virgin's name was Mary. And coming to her, he said, 'Hail, favored one! The Lord is with you.'

But she was greatly troubled at what was said and pondered what sort of greeting this might be.

Then the angel said to her, 'Do not be afraid, Mary, for you have found favor with God. Behold, you will conceive in your womb and bear a son, and you shall name him Jesus. He will be great and will be called Son of the Most High, and the Lord God will give him the throne of David his father, and he will rule over the house of Jacob forever, and of his kingdom there will be no end.'

But Mary said to the angel, 'How can this be, since I have no relations with a man?'

And the angel said to her in reply, 'The holy Spirit will come upon you, and the power of the Most High will overshadow you. Therefore the child to be born will be called holy, the Son of God. And behold, Elizabeth, your relative, has also conceived—a son in her old age, and this is the sixth month for her who was called barren; for nothing will be impossible for God.'

Mary said, 'Behold, I am the handmaid of the Lord. May it be done to me according to your word.' Then the angel departed from her."

Our Lady had grown up in the Temple. She knew the Scriptures. She knew the prophesies about the awaited Redeemer. She might not have known the details of His life before Him, but She knew that the Savior of the world would suffer.

And She said 'Yes.'

Mary said 'Yes' to being the Mother of the Eternal High Priest with all of Her being—with every drop of blood in Her Heart. She did not say, 'Yes, Fiat' surrendering Her body, mind, heart, and will to the Father for just 9 months while the Son of God grew within Her womb, or for just 30 years until He left for His public ministry, or for just 50 or 60 years while She remained on earth. But Mary said 'Yes' to being the Mother of the Redeemer—the Eternal High Priest—for all of eternity.

At the moment of the Annunciation, Mary ceased to be—She handed over Her own personality as 'Mary of Nazareth'—Her desires of being a good embroiderer or simple housewife to Joseph—and She accepted for all eternity to be the Helpmate of God, the Mother of the Redeemer, and the Mother of the redeemed. Her work in helping Jesus in His Priesthood of saving souls began hidden away in that beautiful kitchen garden in Nazareth. In total blind faith as to what details the future held for Her and Her Son, She trusted in God and agreed to accompany Him in His work of saving souls. She gave an unqualified 'Yes'—no exceptions, no 'buts,' no terms or limitations. She accepted this work of Love to accompany Him down the path that would lead inevitably to Calvary. Souls are bought at a price—the price of His Suffering, Blood and Love—and She was willing to partake in that price with Her Son.

On that beautiful Spring day when the angel left Her alone with Jesus' new Body and Heart beating within Her, I am sure Our Lady's mind drifted back to Isaiah 53 and She caught Her breath in a bold act of trust that the One Who entrusted this mission to Her would also carry Her through.

Isaiah 53:1-12

"Who would believe what we have heard?
To whom has the arm of the LORD been revealed?
He grew up like a sapling before him,
like a shoot from the parched earth;
He had no majestic bearing to catch our eye,
no beauty to draw us to him.
He was spurned and avoided by men,
a man of suffering, knowing pain,
Like one from whom you turn your face,
spurned, and we held him in no esteem.
Yet it was our pain that he bore,
our sufferings he endured.
We thought of him as stricken,
struck down by God and afflicted,
But he was pierced for our sins,
crushed for our iniquity.
He bore the punishment that makes us whole,
by his wounds we were healed.

We had all gone astray like sheep,
all following our own way;
But the LORD laid upon him
the guilt of us all.
Though harshly treated, he submitted
and did not open his mouth;
Like a lamb led to slaughter
or a sheep silent before shearers,
he did not open his mouth.
Seized and condemned, he was taken away.
Who would have thought any more of his destiny?
For he was cut off from the land of the living,
struck for the sins of his people.
He was given a grave among the wicked,
a burial place with evildoers,
Though he had done no wrong,
nor was deceit found in his mouth
But it was the LORD's will to crush him with pain.
By making his life as a reparation offering,
he shall see his offspring, shall lengthen his days,
and the LORD's will shall be accomplished through
    him.
Because of his anguish he shall see the light;
because of his knowledge he shall be content;
My servant, the just one, shall justify the many,
their iniquity he shall bear.

Therefore I will give him his portion among the
many,
and he shall divide the spoils with the mighty,
Because he surrendered himself to death,
was counted among the transgressors,
Bore the sins of many,
and interceded for the transgressors."

At the Annunciation, Our Lady knew that the fate of this Child would be Her Own. He was formed from Her Body, took His Blood from Her Own, and their Hearts were knit together in a great 'Fiat.'

From the first seeds of every priest's vocation, the Cross lays its shadow upon his life. To be called to be a priest with Christ, means a call to be a victim. As Jesus was the Victim, the Altar and the Priest on Calvary, He pulls every priest into this mystery of suffering and offering along with Himself. The priest will not come to offer Christ simply exteriorly—but acting *in Persona Christi* Jesus will come to offer Himself from within the ordained man's body, mind, heart, and soul. As the indelible mark of ordination changes the priest man into an image of Christ the Priest, so they are drawn in a mysterious way into Isaiah 53 along with Him. A priest will suffer for his people the way Christ suffered for His people. And those who are called to help the priest along his way—both as intercessors, helpmates and victims offering their prayers, sufferings, and lives for the efficacy of another's priesthood—must do this in imitation of Our Lady, Who was a Mother and Helpmate to Her Son (The Eternal High Priest) as well as to the Apostles and all priests who are drawn into His One Priesthood.

A call to intercede for priests is a call to love as fiercely and selflessly as Our Lady did. It is a call to take upon oneself the burden of the priest—even when not being able to alleviate their suffering, partaking in it in the way that Our Lady partook in Christ's Redemption by standing as a witness, comforter, and support. In agreeing to pray for priests, a soul should imitate Our Lady in the Annunciation—giving a full, trusting "Fiat" to this invitation of God, notwithstanding the knowledge that such an offering may contain a price. And yet, like Our Lady, the soul called to intercede for a priest must trust. Such a soul must take hold of Mary's heroic trust in the Annunciation—keeping in mind that the God Who called them to such a work, will surely give the necessary graces and gifts to help them bring it to fruition. Only with such trust can a soul pray freely and fully along with Mary, "I am the Handmaiden of the Lord. Let it be done to me according to Thy Word."

Visitation

The first work that Jesus did as the Eternal High Priest was from within the womb of His Mother. The first work that Our Lady did as His Helpmate was to carry Him as a

Tabernacle to baptize His tiny cousin within the womb of St. Elizabeth. See here how great the importance of Our Lady in the work of Her Son's Priesthood was. He would be the Victim, but She was the First Tabernacle. She not only gave Him a place to rest His Head (upon Her Pure Heart within Her Womb), but in His great Humility He 'needed' Her to carry Him to St. John the Baptist. And She faithfully did that—notwithstanding the difficulty or length of such a journey for a woman in Her condition. She did not sit at home and brood or worry Herself about St. Joseph. Her act of 'Fiat' was living in active Trust and Obedience as She immediately set out 'making haste' to visit Her cousin. And Scripture writes that not only did Jesus need Her body for His priestly work (to carry Him to St. John the Baptist), but He needed Her voice (so united one with His and penetrated completely by the Holy Spirit) that it was His instrument to touch the heart and soul of little John. Scripture says:

Luke 1:39-56—Mary Visits Elizabeth

"During those days Mary set out and traveled to the hill country in haste to a town of Judah, where she entered the house of Zechariah and greeted Elizabeth. When Elizabeth heard Mary's greeting, the infant leaped in her womb, and Elizabeth, filled with the Holy Spirit, cried out in a loud voice and

said, "Most blessed are you among women, and blessed is the fruit of your womb. And how does this happen to me that the mother of my Lord should come to me? For at the moment the sound of your greeting reached my ears, the infant in my womb leaped for joy. Blessed are you who believed that what was spoken to you by the Lord would be fulfilled."

The Canticle of Mary

And Mary said:
"My soul proclaims the greatness of the Lord;
my spirit rejoices in God my savior.
For he has looked upon his handmaid's lowliness;
behold, from now on will all ages call me blessed.
The Mighty One has done great things for me,
and holy is his name.
His mercy is from age to age
to those who fear him.
He has shown might with his arm,
dispersed the arrogant of mind and heart.
He has thrown down the rulers from their thrones
but lifted up the lowly.
The hungry he has filled with good things;
the rich he has sent away empty.
He has helped Israel his servant,

remembering his mercy,
according to his promise to our fathers,
to Abraham and to his descendants forever."
Mary remained with her about three months and then
returned to her home."

We see here not only that Our Lady was a great Helpmate to Jesus in His First Priestly work of sanctifying St. John the Baptist in his mother's womb, but we also see how Our Lady immediately is drawn up into the act of praise and worship of God that is central to the Priestly Vocation. She, as a good Helpmate, does not draw attention onto Herself. She, instead, 'magnifies' the Almighty—She glorifies HIM—She joins Her Heart to the prayer full of the Holy Spirit's Love beating forth from the Heart of Jesus within Her and this is made visible in the Hymn of Praise She sings in the Magnificat.

This is a great example for us, who strive to imitate Our Lady in aiding priests in their work here on earth. Our job is to be soaked in the presence of the Holy Spirit—to simply allow our hearts to be pure, silent, holy resting places for the Eucharistic Heart of Jesus to repose. And then He will begin to pray and intercede within us for our priest brothers, fathers, and sons. Just as He sprung forth from Our Lady's voice to baptize John the Baptist, He will use our voice in prayer to touch the hearts of the priests for whom we have dedicated our lives to pray and suffer for—

and it will be His work in us with Mary for them. And as miracles begin to happen in priests' lives throughout the world, we can quickly join in Our Lady's Hymn of Praise in the Magnificat—thanking the Father for looking on our small lowliness and doing such a great work through us simply because we placed our unequivocal 'Yes' within the 'Yes' of Jesus and Mary. As we pray for priests we should pray in humility—praying the Magnificat on behalf of them (chosen in great human lowliness to partake in the Priesthood of Jesus) and pray in thanksgiving for the beautiful work that the Lord desires to do through them. In this we always remember, like Jesus' Mother, that we are 'only unprofitable servants' chosen by God in His Mercy to partake in His great plan of the salvation of souls.

<u>Birth of Jesus and His Childhood</u>
<u>Mary as the Mother of the Infant Eternal High Priest</u>

Mary was the Mother of the Infant Priest-Child: To be a priest is to be a victim. So, Jesus—who already was the Eternal High Priest in His Infant state—was destined to be a Victim of Love even from this tender age. Jesus was to be the Bread of Life, so the Holy Spirit arranged for Him to be born when Joseph and Mary were in Bethlehem (a name which means, 'House of Bread.') God used the human thinking and desires of Herod to have a census (which purpose was to increase the taxes of the people) in order to carry out His Own Divine plans. We should never doubt God's Hand even in allowing terrible things at times— because an all-powerful, all-loving God would only allow suffering if He was able to bring a greater good out of it. So, Our Lady found Herself in labor without St. Joseph's having found them shelter. And they ended up in a stable— more like a cave—a place for animals. Their poverty this Holy Night was dire. Joseph hung his mantle at the entrance of the cave to protect his Wife and newborn Babe from the bitter wind. They laid the Baby Jesus in a Manger—the Eucharistic Victim—and although the hay kept Him warm, its pokiness must have foreshadowed the future night when His Innocent Body would be stripped and hung on a Cross. And what did Baby Jesus do? He offered.

He offered.

Even as a Child—His every breath was an offering of love to the Father. As the Divine Word newly clothed in His Mother's Flesh suffering at the hands of fallen man and nature, His Heart never ceased to offer worship, adoration, expiation for our sins. Did this little Babe—Divine Wisdom Incarnate—think upon the children who would be slaughtered in His name (those in Bethlehem as well as those killed in years to come for being His followers, in the name of ethnic cleansing, in abortion in exchange for a life of convenience)? The little Priest was offering that Christmas night. And just as He cried out on the Cross

'Father, forgive them, they know not what they do,' His little voice pierced the cold night air in wordless cries as His Mother hustled to warm Him and get Him to nurse a bit at Her breast.

The first night of adoration: How could Mary and Joseph sleep? Their little Priest King lay sleeping finally warmed by the fire and yet—what did it mean that God had come to earth—and in such poverty, in such humility, in fragility, in hiddenness? No one knew. And then a gentle knock was at the entrance to the cave and a shepherd child, out of breath from running through the fields, whispered a question asking if it was '*Him*'. Could he come in and see the Savior? '*Angels,*' he kept saying, with tears streaming from his eyes... '*Glory to God in the highest and peace to all people of goodwill...*' Slowly behind him came a few more men—trembling with emotion—and one by one they kneeled before the Christ Child to adore their King, their God, their Priest—Victim. A lamb was presented to be placed near to warm the Babe—white like the vestments to be worn by all priests to come. And milk to nourish—food for Him who would become Our Bread of Life.

Never once did Jesus separate the sacrifice from Himself—He was the Priest offering His entire Being in one great act of Love. Men worshiped Him that night—worshiped with Him that night. Every heartbeat of His, every breath He exhaled was in praise of His Maker. And yet not only men, but angels came and sang in the heavens above—'*Glory to God in the Highest and on Earth Peace to people of goodwill.*' Even creation seemed in awe of what was happening in that little cave. A star appeared proclaiming His Presence. The fire seemed gentler and warmer. The wind drew stiller. The animals were no longer smelly and restless—they were overtaken by this Heavenly Presence. And Mary, the Little Mother, with Her arms folded and head bowed, prayed alongside Her Child, Her Priest and Her King.

In our lives God is hidden in the ordinary—hidden sometimes in silence, in poverty, in simplicity. The answers to our prayers are not always immediately visible to our senses. The priests we pray for do not always radiate a regal appearance. Humanity—earth—with its droopy heaviness sometimes presses in. And yet, God is hidden in their presence. God is aware of their needs. God is working in their lives. And God is answering our prayers. Just as the holy Mother did all that was possible to help Her Son, then rested in worship alongside Him, so we are to help those entrusted to our prayer to the degree that we can and then simply offer our presence worshiping the Father with them.

The kings visited the stable in the days that followed— bringing gifts of gold (so fitting for a King), frankincense (to symbolize worship) and myrrh (to foreshadow His death)—also representing how Jesus was to be the Altar (gold), Priest (frankincense) and Victim (myrrh). In all of this Our Lady watched. She prayed and She pondered.

Then came the **Presentation in the Temple**. The little infant Priest was to be offered as a perfect offering to God, His Father. Innocence was pierced—little drops of blood were shed—cries rang out—and a prophesy foretold His destiny. "*This Child will be the cause of the rise and fall of many people—and You Your Heart a sword shall pierce so that the thoughts of many hearts may be revealed.*" (Lk 2:35) Once again the Mother of Jesus' fate is tied up with His Own. If He would suffer, so would Her Heart intertwined one with His. She accepted the sword on behalf of Her Son. Her Love would be as fierce as Her being could muster. We, too, should be prepared to suffer for the priests we love and pray for. To the degree God unites us in heart, in a mission, in life, in prayer—so we will be united in suffering. 'Yes, Fiat, Father," Our Lady answers with every beat of Her Heart. And this 'Fiat, Father, Let it be done...' we pray along with Her.

The Flight into Egypt. We've seen how priests are hated for their witness to Truth. How much more was Truth Incarnate hated? Herod decided to murder all babies in order to get rid of any competition He might have with the Christ Child. And yet, God spared Him through guiding Joseph in a dream to rise and flee immediately into Egypt by night with his little family. So often those priests for whom we pray will be hated—to the degree, at least, that they proclaim the truth. And we must be willing to be hated alongside them. We must be willing to leave all things in this world to rise and go when the Father sends us somewhere. Baby Jesus' comfort on this rough journey was the arms and calming voice of His Mother. So, too, we pray that our prayer and presence interceding before the Blessed Sacrament will comfort those whose priesthoods are full of the shadow of the Cross. And we pray that they always reflect the Truth so brightly that the idols of this world fall down around them, just as the idols in Egypt fell at the arrival of our Infant God.

The Finding in the Temple. Jesus was lost. And Our Lady's suffering was inexplicable. She suffered as a Mother over the impending danger She feared for Her Child. Yet, She also suffered mysteriously an interior darkness of losing Her God. For 12 years, Jesus had been intimately united with Her Heart and Soul—from the first moments of the Incarnation. In addition to Her natural attachment to Her Child, Her Heart had become accustomed to being intimately close to the Heart of God. Can you imagine a life of carrying the Eucharist in your arms or by your side at all times day and night? While Her Son was lost, Our Lady suffered the darkness of the Cross, the exhaustion of Searching, the temptation of doubt, the pain of thirst. Her three days of search mirrored the three hours Her Son would hang on the Cross. She searched for God and cried in Her Heart 'Why have you abandoned me?' She even asked Jesus this question upon finding Him. She, too, cried out 'I thirst'—She thirsted to understand. She thirsted for His Presence. She thirsted for Her God.

And although Our Lady was the perfected woman in this trial, She is somehow also almost like a child in the way that She allows Herself to be taught by Her Child. He teaches Her by His response to Her questions upon finding Him.

> *"When his parents saw him, they were astonished, and his mother said to him, "Son, why have you done this to us? Your father and I have been looking for you with great anxiety." And he said to them,* ***"Why were you looking for me? Did you not know that I must be in my Father's house?"*** *But they did not understand what he said to them. He went down with them and came to Nazareth, and was obedient to them; and* ***his mother kept all these things in her heart."*** (Luke 2:48-51)

She is learning. She is pondering. She prays.

And all the while that Mary is suffering from Jesus' absence, She is partaking in His work without knowing it. Her entire being was always 'Fiat' to God. So, She naturally offered everything—both good and bad—to the Father in union with Her Son. As She suffered having lost Him, Her Heartbeat and Breath prayed 'Fiat'—'I offer all to You'. And in this, Her suffering gives grace for Jesus' words to the priests in the temple (who He remained behind to teach) to be received by them, understood by them and to actually take root in their hearts. Even though Our Lady was unaware of how the Father was using such suffering, the Father was allowing it so that She could partake in the great Mission that Her Son began—even if just as a tiny seed—in the Temple when He was twelve. She was searching for Her child and the priests were searching for truth... both thirsted... and both were answered—by Jesus. She pours out Her soul, but He corrects Her vision. And Mary ponders.

What we can learn in this mystery is how important it is for priests to be humble and to learn from Christ—even when He appears in simplicity as a Child. The priests in the Temple were listening to Him speak—and Our Lady was suffering an absence of Him in order for them to have the grace to understand His Wisdom. As we pray for priests, we too may be asked to feel as if we have 'lost Him' at times. Our thirst, our search, our darkness offered to the Father will be used to give grace to the priests for whom we have offered our lives.

Jesus remained in His Father's house doing His work. And those offering their prayers and lives for priests must allow these men of God to remain in the Father's field. They must pray that worldly cares be shielded from their sensibilities, so that they may truly be focused always on what the Lord has entrusted to them—the 'better part.' Our prayer must create an atmosphere where these men are free to go into the house of God to do His Work.

And after Our Blessed Mother found the Child in the temple, Jesus went back home with Her and Joseph to an ordinary life and obeyed them. I am sure that it was not easy for the Christ Child to remain in the Temple knowing that the parents whom He loved with His entire being were suffering looking for Him. Yet, He obeyed His Heavenly Father's will. He 'learned obedience by what he suffered'. And after fulfilling His Father's will He returned with His earthly parents and remained subject to them. Continuing to grow in humility, obedience, wisdom, and age. At times, priests will be guided by God Himself through the graces of ordination—and at other times they will be guided by men (Bishops and superiors) who are not even as perfect as Mary and Joseph. Yet we must pray that like Jesus, they may always grow in humility and obedience in order to have the discerning wisdom to know the proper response to the various situations presented to them in life.

Chapter 2

Our Lady–the Helpmate of the Eternal High Priest–the Mission of Jesus Crucified

"There is no wine."—It was more than a statement. It was a request.

"There is no wine."—It was about His mission.

"There is no wine."—It was an understanding of souls. The look that Jesus gave to His Mother and the question, *'Woman, what is this between you and Me?'* encompassed much more than the casual bystander could imagine. He called Her "Woman". In Genesis, Adam called Eve 'Woman'. The word 'woman' meant both 'woman' and 'wife.' In calling His Mother, 'Woman,' Jesus' relationship with Her changed. Everything changed in that one request. If the Holy Spirit prompted Our Lady to mother and raise Jesus according to the will of the Heavenly Father in all things, it was this same Holy Spirit who prompted Her request for Jesus to help this married couple. Yet it would be the last request She made of Her Son merely as 'Mother.' With that word 'Woman' Jesus answered Her silent prompting. He agreed. He agreed to allow their relationship to change. He agreed to be the New Adam. He agreed to take Her as His New Eve. The relationship changed. *'What is this between you and Me?'* He asked. He wasn't mocking Her. He wasn't correcting Her. He was simply proposing the question, 'Woman... Woman Who will stand beneath the Cross and watch wine, turned to blood, shed for the world... Woman, Who will crush the head of satan by your obedience... Woman... *Do you know what this is between you and Me? Are you aware of what the Holy Spirit is doing?'* That was the question that Jesus was asking His Mother. ***'Mary, do you know? Do you know what it will mean to be the Mother of the Redeemer? Mary, do you know what it will cost you to be My Helpmate in My mission?'***

Mary's silent glance answered Him. Yes. She knew. The angel proposed to Her 30 years earlier and asked that She become the Mother of God. It was Jesus Himself proposing to Her in Cana. He said, 'Woman... are you willing to drink this cup with Me?' And She, always the wise, obedient handmaiden, said, *'Yes. Fiat. Do whatever He tells you.'* Jesus' mission always cost His Mother. She suffered for Him to bear fruit in the Temple when He remained there at age 12 teaching the priests. And She would suffer in this mission of His public ministry... which ultimately would lead to His death. Jesus would call His Mother 'Woman' again… but it would be under the Cross when He gave Her away to John.

Our Lady lost Her Son in many ways that evening in Cana. She had grown accustomed to 30 years of a hidden life, a private life, alone with Him. And yet She courageously was willing to sacrifice that intimacy to launch Him (and to lose Him) to a public ministry. She would be replaced by the world—regarding the time He spent with Her. And yet their hearts were so intimately united, the greatest pain for Our Mother had to have been that as Jesus was launched into the public, Her Heart would be, too. Jesus went to the crowds who told Him when His Mother drew close. Yet, He would say, 'Who is My Mother? She who does the will of My Heavenly Father…' He knew that His Mother always perfectly fulfilled the will of the Father in heaven. And He was perfecting that love of Hers that was willing to adhere to Him regardless of the cost.

Mary's partaking in Jesus' public ministry meant that She had to be willing to partake in His suffering—people's mockery, misunderstanding and rejection of Him was mockery, misunderstanding and rejection of Her. When they said that He was 'out of His mind,' they were ridiculing Her, His Mother. When Jesus suffered with nowhere to lay His Head… Her Heart ached and bled to be the pillow for His weary brow as it had been for so many years. When He was fatigued, She was exhausted in pain from not being able to feed Him, give Him rest… give Him Love.

And ever looming over His public life was the grave future of the Messiah. Every man, woman, or child whom He healed reminded His Mother of the price He would pay to be that healer… foreshadowed Isaiah 53 where Jesus would be one big gaping wound in order to heal the world. Each word He preached He fed with the sweat of His brow, with pangs of Love from His Heart working and toiling, tilling the land of the hearts of those who were listening to Him. Each sin He forgave had a price that He would pay on Calvary. But Our Lady remained faithfully one with His Heart—at His side from which Her Love was born—every day of His public life and mission.

The priests for whom we pray will have prices to pay for their sacrifice, for the sins they forgive and the people who are healed by encountering Christ's Love from within them. If they have been drawn into Christ's Priesthood, then they agreed to take part in Christ's Pain. And by hiding in Our Lady's Shadow—being willing to be a helpmate to priests the way She was to Jesus and then to all of the Apostles in the early years of the Church—we must be willing to pray as one Heart with Jesus…to endure what He endured…to love (even crucified) as He loved…and to help pay the price of the cost of souls.

"The price of the soul of a priest is very expensive." We, women of the Cross and in the company of Our Lady—as

Her younger sisters in many ways—must agree to love heroically and sacrificially as She did…generously spending our lives to heal the wounds of the world through prayer and sacrifice for those who take Jesus' place. Sometimes we will be called to aid priests as His Mother and other women did—by preparing a meal or cleaning a room. We might be called to teach priests as seminary professors or spiritual guides. We might be called to help them emotionally simply through solid friendships based in grace. But more often we will be called to the battle of prayer…of supporting the work of Jesus' Heart in priests by our daily prayer and sacrifice (often hidden in ordinariness) but offered with a flame of His Heart's Love in the same way His Mother offered all things in union with Him. Our feet may bleed and our clothes may be tattered as we follow Him on this journey. But by offering it for our priest sons, fathers, and brothers, we will be able to fulfill what the Father designed as the role of women in the priesthood— which is to be women of valiant, faithful love who uphold the arms and hearts of the weary through prayer with Mary under the Cross.

Chapter 3

Our Lady–the Gift of the Eternal High Priest–the Passion and Death of Jesus Crucified

*"St. Albert the Great says that the Blessed Virgin was not chosen by the Lord to be a minister, but to be a spouse and help, after the words of Genesis: 'Let us make for Him a helpmate like unto himself." (Gen 11:18) The Most Holy Virgin is not a Vicar (that is to say an instrument), but a coadjutor and a **companion** participating in the reign as She participated in the Passion... the wounds that Christ received in His Body, She felt in Her Heart.*[1]

"What then is the Role of Mary in the Passion? Nothing more than that of a help to Christ, 'a help like unto Himself' as St. Albert the Great says. For Mary is not formally a Priest on Calvary, but only the Associate of the Sovereign Priest. It is by Her union of charity with Christ that She collaborated in

---

[1] Paul Phillippe, O.P., *The Blessed Virgin and the Priesthood* (Chicago: Henry Regnery Company, 1955), p. 36.

the Redemption, it is by Her Immaculate Heart that She is our Mother, as it is by His Sacred Heart that Jesus brought us into life.

"Jesus told St Bridget, 'Her Heart was in My Heart and that is why I can say that My Mother and I have saved mankind as with one Heart, I by suffering in My Heart and My Flesh, and She by the sorrow of the heart and for love.'"[2]

"His is a sacrifice that in the burning fire of suffering consumes within itself the entire godforsakenness of the sinner—and thus it is not only the cost physically but also the most spiritually agonizing sacrifice of all. What, then, is Mary's position now in relation to this divine and human sacrifice?... **She embraces it with Him, since She does not revoke Her Yes (fiat) but remains faithful to it to the last. She lets it be done. She offers to the Father, as She always has done, this self-sacrificing, sacrificial Victim, but in such a way that this offering (oblatio) is for Her the most heartrending renunciation, only thereby making Her oblation truly into a sacrifice, the surrender of what is dearest of all. How much sooner would the Mother suffer in the place of Her Son all that he has to undergo! How terrible**

---

[2] Phillippe, p. 61.

it is to have to assent to this sacrifice, which, from a worldly perspective, is the most meaningless and hopeless of all! And when in Holy Mass, during the Canon, the Church again and again speaks of a sacrifice offered and recalls that it is not only the sacrifice of the Son that is commemorated but that the Church herself fully participates in the act of sacrifice, where else has She truly realized what this Her offering to the Father of the Son, costs Her except at that moment when, in Mary, She offered up Her Son to the Father? Sinners in the Church cannot in fact realize this; they must be glad, rather, that Christ offers Himself for them. And the Church does not exist except in real subjects. Alone, this all-holy Woman, and at most just a few others who have been purified to the point of purest love, can gauge what sword it is that pierces the heart of the Church when She for Her part sacrifices to the Father this self-sacrificing Lamb."[3]

The most excruciating moments of Mary's Motherhood were the most excruciating moments of Jesus' Priesthood. From the first moments that the angel had asked Her to be

---

[3] Hans Urs Von Balthasar, *Priestly Spirituality* (San Francisco: Ignatius Press, 2013), p. 49.

the Mother of the Savior of the World, Mary knew that the cross lay before Her. Our Mother knew Isaiah 53. She knew that the Man of Sorrows would be Christ Jesus Her Son. And She knew that She would be the Mother of Suffering, the Woman of Suffering, the Queen of Suffering as well. And She said 'Yes.'

Those women in the world who complain about not having a place in the Church have completely missed the beauty and dignity of Our Lady's call to be the Mother of Jesus, the Eternal High Priest—and thus through that to be the 'Mother of Priesthoods—the 'Mother of all Priests.' To be the 'Handmaiden of the Lord' would mean to be the servant of a Man-God who came to suffer to redeem humanity. And Our Lady—formed from Christ's side on the Cross—washed and recreated by His Passion and Death and yet receiving this gift applied to Her Alone *earlier in time*—fulfilled Her calling perfectly as the 'New Eve' to 'be 'bone of His bones and flesh of His flesh'. *'What God has united no man may put asunder'*[4] was originally spoken of Her—the Mother in Flesh and Spouse in Spirit of the Redeemer of the world.

Mary was the gift to Jesus par excellence—as well as His 'Helpmate'—offering Her body through His Body (taken completely from Her), Her blood through His Blood (which was formed solely from Her), Her tears with His

---

[4] Mk 10:9

tears, Her Fiat perfectly one with His Fiat to the Father. Jesus not only took Our Lady to Himself on the Cross to recreate and wash Her as a new creation—a perfect Gift to the world of Woman, par excellence—but He shared this gift. He gave Her to us. He gave Her to John.

What was Our Lady's role as the 'Mother and Woman/Wife of the Eternal High Priest'? She united with Him in Body as I said, and united with Him in mind, and united with Him in Heart/Spirit. The Holy Spirit that held Him fast to the wood of the Cross held Her standing beneath Him with Her Heart vulnerably open as a chalice to receive every drop of Blood from this—His con-summated sacrifice of the Mass—into Her being…

And yet Our Lady was not all sorrow. By virtue of the reality of what was happening existentially before Her on Calvary—She saw in Her Heart mysteriously the eternal presence and Divine perspective of what was taking place. She may not have known the details infinitely as God does, but She was acutely aware of the cosmic reality taking place. And so—one with Jesus in body, mind, heart and soul—She offered with Him, She worshiped the Father with Her body, mind, heart, and soul—with Jesus. And if She worshiped through 'fiat' with Her Son, then there was an element of thanksgiving in what was being lived by Her and before Her and with Her (in union with Her Son Jesus—the New Adam).

Our Lady lived a 'twin fiat' with Jesus on the Cross.

It is such a mystery and such a beautiful, deep gift.

Their union of hearts was complete.

What was this Immaculate Heart of Mary and the Sacred Heart of Jesus that were so intimately united on Calvary? What is this that we are called to enter with Mary in our prayer for priests? How could we ever enter it? It is by hiding in Her Heart—as a safe refuge, a garden, a home—that we find our union with Jesus Who first dwelled there in the Incarnation. He was conceived in Mary's Heart as He was conceived in Her Body, and we cannot live in such an atmosphere of Love—the very breath of Her Heart being the Holy Spirit's Love of Fiat—and not be completely consumed by it and transformed by it. As we enter into the mysterious cavern of Mary's Heart, She makes us one with Jesus. She conforms us to His Heart and helps us 'as His body' to 'make up what is lacking in His Sacrifice.' Yes, Jesus consumed the entire chalice needed to save humanity—and yet what was lacking that He could not provide was our own freewill's 'fiat' to partake in that chalice with Him. By going to Our Lady, we are consumed with Her Spirit's perspective of the Sacrifice of the Mass on Calvary—we begin to see with Her eyes, hear with Her ears and pray with Her Heart. Pope John Paul II used to daily pray the prayer *'Totus Tuus ego sum, Maria'* (I am all yours, Mary); *'Et omnia mea tua sunt'* (and all that I am is yours); *'Acceptio me in tua prescencia'* (accept me into your presence); *'Praebe mihi cor tuum'* (Give me your heart).

Give me your heart. That is what the Holy Father would pray. So that he could partake with Mary in Christ's Passion—life and death and resurrection.

We learn to pray in the Heart of Mary, and She takes us to Golgatha to be the teacher of true prayer. It is easy to pray when we are carried away with grace and consolation. But when it is night and the 'Fiat' is hard and all seems lost and senseless—that is when one's heart truly learns to pray. That is the moment where a priest learns to pray *'in persona christi'* at the moment of consecration. And that is the place and moment where we learn to be 'handmaidens' of the Lord—helpmates—standing at the foot of Jesus' Cross and their (the priests') calvaries as well—to worship with them, to strengthen them. What a comfort and strength Jesus must have gained by His Mother's faithful 'Yes' standing foot at the Cross. The encouragement of one who prayed along with Him, for Him—faithful—had to have been an indescribable and unfathomable grace. Their twin fiats invite us to enter into prayer with them as well.

Victims of Love—that is what Jesus and Mary were in this first Mass on Calvary. Jesus gave His Body and Blood to the disciples in the Last Supper—but He was only able to do that because outside of time He had already consummated that sacrifice not only through the Incarnation, but also through the Redemption of His

Passion and death. Every drop of Blood that Jesus shed was Mary's. And the combination of Jesus' Blood and Mary's tears (representing the 'blood of Her Heart') united as ONE to save the world. The new Adam and Eve were totally one in this mystery—united as one in order to give birth to new children—a new humanity.

The night was dark when Jesus prayed, *'Into your hands I commend My Spirit. It is finished,'* and gave up His breath. And yet Our Lady finished His Calvary. The Spirit that carried Jesus' soul into His Father's arms held Mary firm under the Cross. His Love still beat in Her Heart. His blood fell on Her Face as She tasted His pain when blood and water poured from His side. She continued a steadfast fiat waiting... waiting for a word from the Father. Waiting in silence for 'the Word' to rise from the dead.

His body was taken down cold. Empty. How many times had Our Lady felt Her Son's heartbeat as She laid Her hand on His chest? And yet this night purity was dirtied by earth— life was smothered by death—His voice was not echoing. And SHE PRAYED. She continued to pray. His Faith could only remain on earth in Her Heart. If we are all part of the body of Christ, then Our Lady would be the center—the Heart—of His Body. And His body was left alive on earth—IN HER. Both spiritually as well as physically. A mother carries the DNA of her child within her body until the end of her life. So, His tiny Divine Cells—His Eucharistic crumbs—remain hidden in Her

Heart and Womb those three days when He was buried away in the tomb. Oh, Blessed Tabernacle and Faithful servant (never ceasing to worship God regardless of the sacrifice He ordained) was She!!!

Calvary drew silent and yet heaven heard Her breath… 'Fiat,'… 'Fiat'… 'Fiat.'

Chapter 4

Our Lady—the Queen of the Eternal High Priest—the Resurrection, Pentecost, Assumption and Coronation

Our Lady's participation in Her Son's Priesthood did not end with His death. At the foot of the Cross, Jesus extended His Mother's role from being a Helpmate of His Priesthood to being a Helpmate of all priests. *"Standing by the cross of Jesus were his mother and his mother's sister, Mary the wife of Clopas, and Mary of Magdala. When Jesus saw his mother⁻ and the disciple there whom he loved, he said to his mother, 'Woman, behold, your son.' Then he said to the disciple, 'Behold, your mother.' And from that hour the disciple took her into his home."* (Jn 19:25-27) In doing this—in saying this—Jesus was asking Our Lady to be the Helpmate and Mother of all priests. Just as She loved and showed 'compassion'—meaning 'sharing the passion' with Jesus—so, too, would She love and 'suffer with' the millions of priest-sons who would follow in Her Son's footsteps throughout time. Compassion means 'your pain in my heart'. And what a magnanimous Heart and Love

Our Lady must have had to encompass the suffering of the entire world. Our Lady stood as a witness to Jesus—and She would continue to stand as a witness—partaking through worship at the foot of altars all over the world until the end of time.

But before we move on to talk about Our Lady's role in those first moments of the early Church—mothering the apostles and disciples and teaching them—I want to touch upon Our Lady's role as Mother and Helpmate of Jesus, the Eternal High Priest, after the Resurrection and Ascension.

It is obvious, upon reflection, to see Mary's important role in Jesus' Life as a little Embryo within Her, as an Infant, Child, young Adult—even as a Man in His mission to establish the Kingdom of Heaven on earth and then to suffer and die as our Redeemer. Although Christ didn't 'need' His Mother to save the world—in the Father's Wisdom He re-established the natural order 'from the beginning' between man and woman (Adam and Eve) that had been disrupted by sin through the relationship of Jesus (the New Adam) and His Mother (the New Eve). Under the Cross, Our Lady supported Jesus through prayer, through suffering and through love—somehow mysteriously keeping faith and hope and love alive in the midst of the torturous murder of Jesus in diabolical darkness. Even after His death, Our Lady's role was integral in keeping the effects of the Passion alive—the fruits of the Passion planted in the Garden of Her Heart—meritoriously bearing life through Her Fiat in union with His Gift and Sacrifice.

Jesus suffered and poured out His Life to win eternity for humanity—but there is a second part to redemption of mankind that is not dependent on Jesus' perfect gift to us alone. He lived the ACTION of saving—but humanity was still free to use their freewill in the RECEPTION of that gift. The gift could only have merit for mankind if mankind chose to receive it. That is the mysteriously wonderful place that Our Lady encompassed in the measure of human history. **She alone was the perfect tabernacle—totally and perfectly receiving and treasuring and protecting Her Son's gift of redemption to humanity so that others could come to the well of Her Heart and gaze within, learning how to imitate this reception.** Adam gave life to Eve—and Eve had to receive it for it to take root. In the same way, Jesus gave new life to humanity—but humanity had to receive that life for it to take root and transform the soul. Mary modeled for all of humanity—and even more than that—through Her reception She won the grace for others to partake in this reception with Her. As a Mother, She nursed Her spiritual children down through the ages with Her Own Heart's fiat—in the Incarnation, but also at the foot of Her Son's Cross—as He lived on earth a timeless Mass as Priest, Altar, and Victim in order to rewash and recreate humanity. Through all His suffering, He purchased heaven for us. And through Her Suffering, His Mother stooped down to us, Her creature children throughout the ages, to teach us how to drink of His medicine of Love.

The moments after Jesus breathed His last on Calvary, His Mother waited with the eternal light of the Holy Spirit beating within Her Heart as a vigil lamp. Just as in a church the red vigil lamp tells the people that Christ is truly present in the Blessed Sacrament, so from the moments of Jesus' conception within Mary the Light of God's Love in Her eyes told people that His little Heart was beating under Her Chest, within Her womb. As Jesus received all of His humanity from His Mother, it was Her blood that He shed on Golgatha. And yet that same blood did not cease to flow through Her veins even after it was drained from His Heart by a spear. A mother carries the DNA of Her children within her body all of the days of her life, so even if Jesus' Sacred Heart had stopped beating when He gave up His Spirit to His Father, part of His Body was still living (as little cells) within the womb and heart of Mary. And as Jesus was taken down from the Cross and placed—cold, dead, lifeless—in the embrace of His Mother, Our Lady's Heart beat fiercely with Faith and Hope in addition to Her Heart's extravagant Love—as a vigil light speaking to the world through Her silence, Her presence, Her gentle tears that God was still with them. His body was in Her Arms, and His breath (which had made Him incarnate within Her 33 years prior) was still within Her soul. Our Lady was a Helpmate to Jesus, the Eternal High Priest, in this way—in each moment that passed as She waited for His Resurrection—simply by being united to Him as He entered the abode of the dead to free the souls of the just into Heaven. Somehow His Spirit—the Holy Spirit of Whom Mary was completely full of—beat forth in union with Her Heart, out from Her Heart to give the light of anticipation, of Hope, of Faith, of direction to those left in utter darkness and despair around Her. Mary's Love and prayerful worship called forth the Savior of the world from heaven in the Incarnation—and Her 'Yes' to the angel enabled Him to take Flesh. It was similarly Her Love and prayerful worship after His death on the Cross that prayed for the Savior of the world to rise from the Dead and to renew the earth that had been bathed by His Precious Blood. Jesus was the Eternal High Priest-Victim slaughtered and buried in a tomb, and His Mother was His Helpmate, soaking up His Blood from the Calvary Hill and treasuring His Presence within Her Heart as She awaited the resurrection of all.

A Holy Saturday Lament with Mary…

Oh sweet Mother Mary,
Your heart is like a tomb…
For your Love, your Life has been crucified!
Death—His Death on the Cross—seems to consume
    all space and time.

The Spirit making you one—Who enfleshed within
   your womb
-gave human life to the very Word of God—
seems to be buried in the tomb of silence this long
   day.
Cold body—frozen in death.
All life poured out by the lance in His side.
Emptiness—numbness—silence
What would you give, dear Mother—your very life
   and heart—to hear His breath on Calvary once
   more?...
Altar and victim consumed in the flames of love
-and all that is left on earth is the ashen flesh of
   your heart awaiting....
Yes, waiting alone—enduring deeper than even
   Golgotha's pain
-where union with your Son gave beat to your
   bleeding heart...
Waiting alone speaks ... lives... hopes...

Mary, let me wait with you—for nothing but the life
   of your Son
...could give breath to my suffocating prayer this
   day...
Mary, let me wait in you
-in hope—without His fire
-in faith—without His light

-in love—without the warmth of His presence

Only in you—from whom His flesh came forth—
   can I find a seed of meaning for existing today...
Heaven seemed to die this day...
For Jesus—our only path to the Father—has died!
   Has died!
And left only the silent, still, empty, dark, cold
   Heart pierced by our sin—locked in a tomb—
   and guarded from our kisses by suspicion....
Oh never would that Eucharistic gift mean more
   than on this day—when Love and Life is buried
   away in a tomb in wait...
   Oh Love—locked in the tabernacle of the
   Father's will in wait... hear and answer my
   longing heart for Your return in glory!!
The only memory of His goodness is His death—
   death on the Cross
Which spoke final words of forgiveness and
   ultimate surrender.
Oh Mary, pray with me, in me, for me... teach me
   the art of waiting in hope this day.
For my breath expired yesterday at 3:00 and my
   heart has no tears left to weep...
My prayer is numb, empty silence.
Silence—holding hope—make my heart reflect your
   Own, dear Mother—for you remember the

Father's promise—speak to my darkened memory—prepare and cleanse me for the gift of His redeeming Love resurrected tomorrow.

What a long, crushing night this Holy Saturday weighs—heavy in my soul!...

Yes, tomorrow—the Easter shadows peeking through the wilted flowers on Calvary—soaked by His blood—will overcome the darkness, the silence of this empty day of death.

But how shall I endure the silent wait today?

Sweet Mary, pray for me... teach me to wait in silence full of hope.

Holy Saturday—a day without light—a life without breath—a prayer empty of meaning as the soul of my Beloved has gone from earth!

Three days in a tomb—three hours on a cross—one suffering between the Mother's Heart and Yours—sweet Jesus—to whence have You gone?

Heaven speaks not of Your resurrection yet on this day following death—and yet earth sees Your breath no more....

"Pray and wait... hope and believe... and love in the silence enduring..."

Those were Your instructions for this heaviest of days lived in union with Your Mother's lonely, abandoned heart of fiat.

Today I have no blood to offer prayer—no pain, for
　　stillness consumes all.
Beat, my heart! Believe, my hope! Beat on in hope,
　　my faith! Love enduring unto—and through this
　　night of awful death.
Mary, hold me and let not my heart's life stop
　　beating…
His Love enflames my love and yet it seems to have
　　died.

From the grave He speaks in the echo of Psalms:
"I waited, waited for the Lord;
who bent down and heard My cry.
Drew Me out of the pit of destruction
Out of the mud of (man's sin)—of the swamp
Set my feet upon rock, steadied my (newly born,
　　resurrected) steps.
And put a new song in My mouth
A hymn to our God
Many shall look on in awe
And they shall trust in the Lord."

My heart trembles as it waits for the earthquake of
　　tomorrow morning's resurrection song!
Holy Spirit—hide no more—come and pray within
　　me in my wait with the Mother.
-We put our hope in You…

Sweet Jesus, locked in the Garden—please rise and
call my name!

"Fiat! Fiat! Fiat!"—somehow my heart beats tucked
between the Mother's and Yours…

Father, have mercy on Your child today and answer
my prayer…

Amen. +[5]

Mary in union with Her Son—the Eternal High Priest— in the Resurrection, Ascension, and Pentecost

Mary withdrew to Her room and She waited—in
adoration of the Lord She no longer could behold—like the
most faithful of souls still for hours before Christ's
Eucharistic Presence in Adoration in years to come—She
waited, adoring. She lived an act of Hope with the
confidence of Faithful Trust led by Her Heart's Love. This
was not a time for Our Lady to think or speak or act for or
in union with Her Son. It was a time for Her to wait still—
almost as dead and locked away in a tomb along with Her
Christ Child—listening attentively for the Voice of Her
Father in Heaven to call His Son forth in the Resurrection.
And once Jesus would step forth in His Resurrected Love

---

[5] April 7, 2012

and Presence on earth, Our Lady would be drawn forth from Her waiting prayer along with Him. When the Divine Life of the Holy Spirit would be breathed into the nostrils of our Sleeping Lord, the same breath of life would lift Our Mother's dormant, dying Heart. It was Her union with Jesus' Heart—as His Heart began to beat again—that lifted Our Mother off the floor of Her room in patient adoration and waiting. A Heart so one with Her Son was surely the first place Jesus ran for refuge and to restore Strength and Life once He was risen from the dead. In a nanosecond of time Christ lifted His Mother from prayer in an embrace of Love that transfigured Her Heart as it invigorated Her Body. In a way, Our Mother had died with Her Son and rose again with Him through their union of Love. Yet Christ was not to physically remain with His Mother on earth after His Resurrection—He was to appear to the others and then ascend to the right hand of His Father in Heaven while leaving Her for a time on earth to mother the rest. The Light of Jesus' Resurrected Presence filled Our Lady with His regal majesty and Priestly power because of the union of Their hearts of Love. And Our Lady was to continue to be a Mother to His Priesthood by remaining with His Apostles on earth and mothering them (as they lived *in persona Christi* His sacerdotal gift.)

It is an incredible thing to meditate on how Our Lady continued to live in union with Her Son, the Eternal High Priest, as He appeared to the others in His Resurrection.

The flame in Her Heart standing witness to His Presence on Earth and announcing His Love must have grown exponentially each time He appeared to His Apostles, the Disciples, and His women friends—each time He reached out to recreate and heal their wounds from the Passion into jewels of Resurrected Love. She lived that mystery of recreation with Him simply through Her 'Fiat'. Mary's Fiat that brought forth the Word of God from Heaven to be incarnate in Her womb, Mary's Fiat that surrendered to the Father's plan for Her Son's life for 33 years, including His cruel betrayal, torture, and death, was the same Fiat to the Father's will that shared in His joy of the Resurrection which gave life to all others around Her. Just as Mary 'helped' Her Priest-Son by receiving the fullness of His gift of Redemption into the tabernacle of Her Heart, so, too, She 'helped' Her Priest-Son by receiving the fullness of His Resurrected Love which sparkled from Her eyes and glowed from Her skin. Christ came to suffer, die, and rise from the dead to recreate His Father's fallen Creation. And Mary was the perfect, immaculate receptor ('wife') who received His gift. For this reason, She is the model and archetype of Christ's 'Bride,' the Church. In these moments of the Resurrection, Our Lady radiated the words of Revelation 21:9 *"Behold the Bride, (the 'Woman'), the Wife of the Lamb!"*

As Christ proceeded to ascend into Heaven, He drew His Mother's Heart—as the New Eve and *'Bone of His*

Bones and Flesh of His Flesh and Spirit of His Spirit—into heaven with Him. He drew it through Love. It is a bigger miracle of grace that Our Lady did not ascend into heaven with Jesus—yet remained on earth to pray with, teach, and serve the Apostles—then it is that She was later Assumed Body and Soul to reign with Him. We are all one body with Christ—and Mary was the perfection of this never having sinned to separate Her from Him. And as His Body and Soul was pulled into Heaven to reign with His Father, Mary's Heart began to bask in a new way in His Heavenly Presence and Light. Seemingly impossible for such a Woman to grow in holiness or union with Her Son, and yet Her radiant oneness with Him increased as She fiated to remaining on earth to love and serve Him in His little priest brothers before joining Him forever. Once Our Lady was assumed into Heaven, She continued to assist at the Perpetual Liturgy of Her Son's Gift and Reign as Eternal High Priest simply by Her Presence, Her Obedient surrender to His Will, Her Love, Her Faith, Her Hope which She exercises not only by Her Heart's Worship, but also by interceding for us left here on earth. Mary as Mother and Helpmate of Jesus, the Eternal High Priest in Her Assumption and Coronation (as Queen) is a role that She lives in absolute purity and humility—being perpetually and perfectly filled by God—united with Him in Heaven… and yet this union isn't stagnant—it gives life to us here on earth.

Mary was a true Mother and Helpmate to Jesus, the Eternal High Priest, through serving those drawn into His priesthood *'in persona Christi'* by ordination. And it is there where we find our place in joining Her in loving and serving Him. We see how Our Mother gathered the bewildered disciples into the Cenacle to pray with hearts open, full of faith and hope for the coming of Christ's Love in the fullness of the Holy Spirit. Mary had already called the Word from heaven in the Incarnation through such faithful, longing prayer... and She had already called to Jesus for His Resurrection from Death by such ardent, hopeful thirst. It was natural for Her to embrace this final coming of His Presence through the Gift of the Holy Spirit to the Church with a Heart completely consumed with the same longing, faith, hope, and open, docile love.

And this time She had students...this time She had new sons...this time She was more active of a Mother teaching the early Church than any work She had to do for Jesus. For years, She had joined Him in His work—yet He was God and perfect. Our Lady's new Cross was to teach and form and help fallen men to reach the heights of sanctity that She knew in Her Wisdom that the Father had destined for them. Our Mother did not fold Her hands and tell the Apostles a formula of words that they needed to recite in order to receive the Holy Spirit. Instead, She showed them the witness of a stance of heart—She radiated a presence that infused into them grace through Her Love union that was ever growing with Christ in Heaven—and the grace that exploded from Her (the 'Woman' already full of grace and the Holy Spirit) inspired these men to open their hearts, to receive healing and love, and to be prepared for 10 days before heaven exploded the fullness of its gift upon them.

Yes, I am sure in the days of the early Church Our Lady was a helpmate of Her new priest sons through cooking and cleaning and encouraging… but most of all She was present to them by inspiring them with Her open, pure, attentive Heart at each Mass they prayed. Her prayer ministered to them. She was the receptacle that taught these 'givers' how best to guide the souls entrusted to them. If Our Lady is the Mediatrix of all Grace—meaning that God chose in His Wisdom to give to the world all the Graces that come through Christ through Mary (whose yes in the Annunciation incarnated Him into this world), then She also was an instrument to give birth to the Holy Spirit's Presence among the early Church (and even up to this day). She, who was the Mother of Christ the Head, continues to be the Mother of Christ the body. And it is Her Faith, Hope, and Love that give birth to our eternal salvation… not because of Her Herself but because She is the aqueduct—the instrument—through which these gifts of Jesus Christ and His Holy Spirit come to us. For this reason, every priest and every soul that prays for priests needs Mary.

Chapter 5

In the Shadow of Our Lady–Entering Her Spirituality of Praying for Priests

And now, after meditating upon Our Lady's place as the Mother and Helpmate of Jesus the Eternal High Priest throughout all of His life here on earth and His glory in Heaven, as well as Her help to His little 'priest sons' down through the ages, we turn to our role in this mystery. How can a soul live in 'the Shadow of Our Lady'? How can we not only look at and exteriorly imitate, but also interiorly come to live united as one with Her the spirituality She lived of praying for priests?

We have to look a little deeper yet at the interior dispositions of Our Lady's Heart in this ministry. We not only have to be inspired by Her witness and Love and strive to conform our lives to Her life with Jesus, but we also have to allow our hearts to be set aflame with the same fire of the Holy Spirit's Love as Hers was. This will make our hearts soft and malleable. We have to 'lean' our hearts up against Hers so that by pressing upon Her Love we come to conform our will, our thoughts, our desires, our intentions, our entire beings to that of Her Heart's Love. We must allow Her to press Her 'Fiat' within our souls—so that we can pray this along with Her—a 'Fiat' for the Father's will to be done in our lives and the lives of those priests for whom we pray. This is how we can imitate Her Motherhood—by giving all to the Christ Child Whom we invite to live within us—and then by loving and supporting His presence in the lives of those priests who the Lord brings to our lives.

Every child is like their mother. At least if the child spends most of his or her time with that mother. And it is very important for young children to have the presence of their mother at all times—because they learn more from their mother's presence to them than from their mother's actual words or instruction to them. Children are always observing, and in innocence they imitate that which is around them. Their facial expressions, their words, their ways of doing things naturally follow those of the mother who cares for them day and night when they are young. In today's world, traditional roles have been changed a bit—sometimes fathers or a grandparent or another caretaker ends up taking this place that God originally designed for mothers—and what results is that the child begins to imitate these people instead. More than all else, a child is formed by love—by the love oozing from the presence, the voice, the caress of his/her mother throughout the day. It's in the normal things of life imbued with his/her mother's love that form and transform a little person into the adult he or she someday will be. All of this is true for human children and relationships, and all the more it is true of our spiritual relationship with Mary, Our Mother and Our Queen.

We are to be conformed to Jesus Christ in all things— and Our Lady's job as our heavenly Mother is to do that. She is so perfectly immaculate—so humble and pure and docile and surrendered in obedience and trusting of Our Lord—that He always was able to fill Her completely and fully form Her into Himself. She was then given to us to form us through love to conform unto Her Heart, which in turn makes us conform to the heart of Christ. It is literally by following his mother around like 'a little shadow' that a child learns—absorbs—every gesture, word, and attitude of her presence. In the same way we—as Our Lady's little children—must follow Her around as a little shadow to absorb Her way of thinking, of praying, of acting, of speaking, of working, of loving and even of resting—in and with and for Jesus. It is a great grace of the Holy Spirit to allow us to be so close to Two Hearts that are so pure and holy. And it is an even greater gift that we are allowed to be drawn into their Love and partake of it in some little way. By imitating Mary, we learn how to best love Jesus. And together with them we learn how to best love Jesus in each other—and specifically in His priests.

What do we learn from Our Lady? Mary was the Mother of Jesus and is the Mother of all priests—and we must imitate Her in that. A motherly love is an attentive love—a selfless love—an all-consuming love. That is how we are called to love Jesus, the Eternal High Priest.

We are called to be totally attentive to Him—to His thoughts, words, actions, desires, prayers. Sometimes, this is done directly—almost mystically—but more often it is done by being attentive to and serving His Presence in those around us, and in His priest sons. A spiritual mother to priests will sometimes see a need and be called to fill it— a lonely priest needing a place to spend a holiday will find comfort in a warm meal and cup of coffee around the fireplace at her home. A priest may need a friend with whom to share his thoughts, dreams, and desires. A priest may need help with laundry or with cleaning the church or some other project. And a woman may be a 'mother' to him by filling in this way. But much more often a woman will be called to love and serve her spiritual priest sons through prayer. She will be called to that attentiveness to the Holy Spirit that Our Lady always treasured in Her Heart that hears the Holy Spirit knocking on her heart's door when a priest is in trouble and needs prayer, needs sacrifice.

A woman is called to be selfless—for rarely will her prayerful devotion be easy. An old adage, which some attribute to St. Thérèse of Lisieux, goes like this: 'The price of the soul of a priest is very expensive.' Such a true statement! If it was St. Thérèse who said it, she knew very well what kind of sacrifice her motherly (and sisterly) love and friendship to priests would cost—for it cost her her life. Selfless love may even be unrequited. Priests are so busy that the one who prays for them may not receive much attention or help back in return. Mothers are rarely appreciated for all that they do for their children—and spiritual mothers are even less appreciated, for they don't have the physical bond that demands respect from their children. It is much easier for a spiritual child to forget, neglect, and run away from his spiritual mother than for a physical child to forget, neglect, and run away from his parent.

A spiritual mother's love—in imitation of Our Lady— will be called to live an all-consuming love for their priest sons. This entails being so united with Jesus, the Eternal High Priest and Victim—that they are drawn up into His very sacerdotal Love. Just as Our Lady was united as one Heart with Her Son to the point that Her Heart was pierced by the swords and thorns that pierced His Own, so too a spiritual mother of priests will share in this all-consuming victim sort of love. They will do that to console and be a helpmate to Jesus in His Priesthood and work in the salvation of souls—but He will sometimes allow for her to share in this with and for a particular priest on earth as well. And sometimes for multiple priests.

As the soul is drawn up into this all-consuming love of Christ with His Mother on Calvary for souls, He may share the specific sufferings of particular priests with the soul in order to unite them through His priesthood and to allow the soul's divine love for the priest to take on some of the burden of his own victimcy. A call to the priesthood is a call to a life of suffering with Christ for the salvation of souls, and just as Our Lady (and others) helped Jesus through compassion and uniting with His sacrifice in love, so too at times Christ may call a spiritual mother under Our Lady's Shadow to also be drawn into this com-passion with Her for specific priests.

Mary was the Helpmate of Jesus, and She is the Helpmate of all priests. We must imitate Her in that. Our Lady did not only live with and support Jesus in His Priesthood on earth, but She was left behind after His Resurrection and Ascension to give the same attentive care to the Apostles and disciples left behind on earth to begin His Church. In some ways Our Lady was formed in being a spiritual Mother to all priests through Her attentive care and love in helping Her Son (both physically, as well as spiritually). And after being 'trained' as His Helpmate, She was entrusted with the difficult task of being the Helpmate of those drawn into His priesthood—those sons who were less than perfect and yet chosen by the Father to share in His One eternal Priesthood. Under the Cross, Jesus assigned this task to His Mother through St. John—and He continued to pour out the gifts She needed to be attentive, selfless, and all-consuming through love to the needs of these men. Because She already lived this role perfectly with Jesus, in some way She drew forth the graces these priest-sons needed from their hearts by Her Presence and Love.

Mary was a *Gift to Jesus* and She is *a Gift of Jesus to priests.* We must imitate Her in that. Mary's gift was not for one moment or a few years, but it extended throughout Her life and into eternity. Our imitation of Her Love for Christ, the Eternal High Priest, must strive to match Hers. Jesus was a total gift to us, and we must respond with a total gift of ourselves. This will be lived directly with Him, but at times He may call souls to gift themselves back to Him through one of His priests or for one of His priests. If a spiritual mother is awakened at 3am with a priest on her heart, she must get up and pray... he may be experiencing temptation, doubt, or despair. Or he may have needs (to grow in virtue), and the Lord can only pour out grace on him while he sleeps because he is less resistant to changing his ways at this time. A woman may receive a headache, and it will be a call to offer it for the discernment, protection, and needed graces of wisdom for one of her priest sons/brothers. She must be a gift to his specific needs as if it were the Savior Himself crowned with thorns standing before her. A call to enter spiritual maternity (or paternity for that matter) of priests is a call to be so intimately united to and surrendered to Jesus Christ's

Priesthood, Love, and Plan that one is willing to be immolated as a victim in the way that the Father allows for whoever He desires. This is complete, dedicated, and selfless love. Of course, God created us for relationships, and He would want for a priest to receive and respond in kindness to such a gift from a soul. But even when a priest is wounded or selfish or aloof, the Lord desires for the spiritual mother to be faithful and to depend on Him to work things out. It is the greatest suffering to suffer for, pray for, and love those who completely reject or ignore your love—and yet such love is the most selfless, pure, and divine that exists on earth.

Mary is the Queen of Jesus the Eternal High Priest, the Queen of all priests—and we must imitate Her in that. Our Lady reigns through Love. She loves so much that Her children are melted by Her Love and filled with a desire to obey what She deems best for their lives simply because it is impossible to refuse such utter, pure, and holy Love. We are called as spiritual mothers to be drawn into that Love until we become part of it—an opaque vessel through which it flows to others—specifically priests. Our Lady's authority is one of Love, and we may be partakers in wielding that authority only to the degree that we enter into the Wisdom and Love of Her Heart—which is perfectly united to the Wisdom and Love of the Father. By our treasuring the priests entrusted to our prayer within our heart as we dwell with Mary, we will prayerfully help them conform more closely to Christ through the closeness they have to us. Mary is the Queen of Jesus, meaning that He is the King. She obeys Her King in all things, and together they decide what is best for their subjects. By entering their relationship in Love, we are allowed to partake of their kingdom, and this entails always conforming our lives, our wills, and our desires to that of Our King and Queen. What better service can we give to priests than to draw them through prayer and love into this bath of Divine surrender to the Father's will in everything? Immediately upon entering the chambers of Mary and Jesus' united Hearts, we are purified, humbled, and made holy. And in that, there is great power to be an instrument of grace to the priests entrusted to us and to those who they serve.

Chapter 6

Spirituality of Praying for Priests—as Spiritual Mothers, Sisters, and Daughters

In order to be a spiritual mother, sister, and daughter of priests in such a way that helps them fulfill their priesthood in holiness, we must first become ourselves conformed to Jesus the Eternal High Priest as His mother, sister, and child. We do this by being baptized and washed by grace in this Sacrament, thus making us part of His family. We do this by the Sacrament of Confession—removing any and all obstacles that separate us from God and receiving (and then returning) the fullness of His Love. We do this by Confirmation where we are drawn into the fullness of the Holy Spirit's gifts, designs, and fruits for us. We do this by the Mass—by receiving the very Body, Blood, Soul, and Divinity of Christ into our bodies and souls. And next to these sacraments, the greatest way that we can become transformed by Christ and conformed into His Heart is by spending time with Him—specifically in adoration of His Eucharistic Presence. In this time, we are resting our heads on His Heartbeat the same way that St. John did at the last supper. And His Heartbeat speaks to us of His Love, of His Correction, of His Grace. This time we spend with Him will be different for each soul. Some may grow by meditation on and praying the Rosary. Others will grow by reading and meditation on Scripture or some other Church/saint's writing. Others will grow by resting with Him in a love union of silence. Others might grow by speaking to Him directly from one's heart. But most important to conforming us to Christ is to spend that time with Him in the Blessed Sacrament. There He teaches us how to Love and forms us to be the saints we were created to be. Only after this time with Him are we able to go out and serve and love Him through what we do, what we say, what we suffer and how we pray actively in the world. We must have this time of rest and reception of His Love in order to then have something to go out and live actively in union with Him.

Once we have become accustomed to living in union with Mary and Jesus as the Eternal High Priest, we will be asked to live this with and for their priest sons in the world. There are many ways that a soul can be called to serve and love the priesthood. And each way will vary immensely according to one's state in life, responsibilities, spirituality, and ultimately the will of God. A mother will be called never to neglect her own children to pray for and care for priests. How sad it would make Jesus for a mother of a large family to neglect her children, brothers, or sisters in order to have a special relationship with some priest. God calls us to first live holiness with those He has especially entrusted to us, and by living and offering that up priests are helped.

On the other hand, a consecrated woman or religious will be called to sacrifice their own families at times to aid in the work of priests. Their help is direct, the same way that many of the women in the Gospel were called to serve the apostles. A mother must split her heart between her husband and children and any mission she might feel to pray for priests. By loving those in her family around her (parents, siblings, children, etc.) and offering that for priests, she helps them best. But there are also souls who have been called to give up family relationships in order to more fully enter into the spirituality of praying for, suffering with, and serving priests.

In the missions, I was asked to give up everything to make sure that the priests were fed, had clean clothes, and provided for spiritually so that they could bear the proper fruit as the Lord desired. Many times as a mother and sister to priests, I was asked to meet with women needing help, since these women did not understand the appropriate relationship between priests and lay people as I did. By helping them (and thus taking this burden from the priests), I was able to protect these men. In this I was truly being their sister—a grace I was given because of my hours of prayer, but which the women in Russia did not understand.

This is where what I wrote before comes into play—the upmost importance of a soul called to pray for priests to spend more time with Jesus than they do with the priests themselves. They are ultimately called into a Love relationship with Christ, the Eternal High Priest. They are called to be consumed with His Suffering, His will, His Sacrifice, and His Love—and it is only then through and with Him that she is called to suffer for, serve, and love His priest sons. This is why one's own spiritual life of Confession, Mass, and daily adoration is so important in the work of praying for priests. The more one is consumed with Christ, the more efficacious her prayers will be for His priest-sons. The closer she draws to Our Lady and Her Humility, Purity and Wisdom, the more she will inspire her priest sons (whether she has actual physical contact with them or not) to be inspired by and drawn into such holy humility, purity, and wisdom. We become what we contemplate, so it is by thinking about Our Lady and Her Son's relationship in this—and by spending time with Them and allowing Them to draw us into this relationship through grace and love—that we become the best instruments to pray for and suffer for priests. In essence, we end up offering Their offering instead of our own. The more we drink in adoration with Jesus, the more we will be able to pour out His grace and love.

Practical Ways of Prayer

Besides literal adoration of Jesus the Eternal Priest in the Blessed Sacrament, there are many other ways that a soul can live in union with Our Lady's prayer for priests under the Cross and in the Cenacle at Pentecost.

- One can go and sit before His presence and simply offer that simple prayer of presence as a portal of grace for a particular priest.
- One can pray the rosary for her priest sons and brothers, and thus wrap them in the mantle of Our Lady's Love.
- One can meditate on St. Joseph and pray to him for priests. He was the most perfect servant of Christ and a great model for all men to know how to live in passionate purity, total obedience, the utmost humility, meekness, gentleness, strength, righteousness, courage, patience, attentiveness, kindness, wisdom, and generosity.
- One can pray to the other saints for priests—specifically focusing on those who had a similar vocation to pray for priests (asking St. Thérèse, for example, to intercede for them) or focusing on those who were holy examples of priests themselves.
- One can focus on praying for specific virtues that the Lord puts on one's heart for them (praying for

faithfulness, wisdom/prudence, humility, purity, obedience, gentleness, strength, prayer, preaching, administration.)

- One can pray through the scriptures, placing the priest in the Gospel in the place of Peter, Matthew, John, James, or Simon and asking the Lord to grant them the graces that He granted His first Apostles.

- One can ask for the prophetic gift of knowing what a priest needs to be prayed for…and then pray for whatever comes to one's heart.

- One can also just offer things for his intentions, needs, protection, and personal growth while mortifying one's own curiosity as to what specifically those things are. This is a most perfect way of love and detachment. By accepting obscurity in one's prayer, you are protecting the priests who you pray for—leaving their hearts in a safe environment of hiddenness with the Lord.

- One can be very practical in prayer and pray for the priests' personal growth in holiness, his family, his friends, his relationships, his talents, his weaknesses, his parish, his religious house, his finances, the groups he runs, those whose confessions he hears, who marriages he counsels, who he anoints, who attends his Masses and listens to his preaching, whose funerals he serves, for his own health or his needs/intentions (whether one knows the specifics about these things or not).

- One can read about and meditate on the holiness of the priesthood and offer that prayer/meditation/ reading for a specific priest to receive the grace needed to live it.

- One can offer one's prayers, works, joys, sorrows, and sufferings throughout the day for a priest through a morning offering. Little things with much love weigh heavily in the heavenly scales. One can offer the 5ᵗʰ dirty diaper they change or the temper tantrum of a child as a sacrifice of love for a priest.

- One can fast and offer greater sacrifices (sleeping on the floor, being cold, giving up food, etc.) as an act of love for a priest.

- One can actually offer to the Lord to take on the sufferings of a priest. There have been cases when one who authentically and purely loves a priest with and for Christ has been allowed by Jesus to feel the priests' suffering and pain and to offer it with him— whether it be his sadness, his fear, his doubt, his temptations, his cancer, his sickness, his exhaustion. Just as Simon of Cyrene was allowed to lift the Cross from Christ's back for a while during the Way of the Cross, at times the Lord allows certain souls who have been trained deeply in His Own Love to take on the sufferings of others in this more concrete way. Often, others are left unaware of what others are suffering for them.

- The most efficacious way to pray for priests is at the Eucharistic Sacrifice of the Mass. This is the way that Our Lady prayed most powerfully with and for Jesus. She stood one victim with Him—one in body, mind, heart, soul, and spirit—offering His Sacrifice on Calvary. By going to Mass and joining in with the priest and Christ's sacrifice through him, one can offer the most powerful of graces to the priests for whom one prays. No prayer is more powerful than a Mass. When one is prevented from attending Mass, one can always turn one's heart to the altars throughout the world where Mass is taking place (each second four chalices and four hosts are offered in consecration somewhere in the world) and unite one's entire life with Jesus' Offering on those Altars, which is His Offering on Calvary. In this way one is bathing a priest in His Blood, and Jesus' Blood heals all, converts all, transforms all, inspires all, guides all, and enflames all uniting a priest's soul with His Own.

For Whom Should We Pray?

It is a good practice to pray for the priests who serve us on a regular basis—as an act of kindness for their sacrifice and dedication, as well as asking for the grace for them to be open to the Holy Spirit in the Confessional and while preaching at Mass. Yet, the Lord calls some people into a more intense vocation of praying for priests in general, or even for specific priests that they know. They may be asked to pray extra prayers or days of the week for priests at their parish, priests who administered the Sacraments to them (those who baptized, confirmed, anointed, married, ordained someone and those who hear our confessions and sacrifice the Mass.) We should pray for those who buried our loved ones who have died and those to whom we are bound by duty (relatives, friends, and those the Lord has specifically pointed out to us needing prayers). We should pray for priests who have hurt us by words or actions (or omissions in serving as Jesus would desire), those who are most struggling, those in authority, those in the public light. We should pray for priests with whom we have served in a mission or a work, those who suffer the most and the sick and dying. We shouldn't even neglect priests who have died or left the priesthood—we pray for their hearts to find peace and healing through union with God. We should pray for any priest that the Lord puts on our hearts and, for some, it will be a commitment to pray for their priesthoods for the rest of our lives.

What are the Personal Fruits of This Ministry?

It would not be right to conclude this chapter without touching briefly on the fruits and benefits that a soul inevitably enjoys when she or he has embraced a vocation to pray and suffer for priests. Yes, such a life is united with Jesus, the Eternal High Priest on the Cross, so it is not easy. Such a soul will have her heart pierced right along with Our Mother's on Calvary. And yet, the work of praying for, suffering for, and serving priests is not a human work. It is not a work even like a mission or family life that can be based on human personalities and friendship. It is a work of Divine Love. It is a graced friendship—one based in God, imbued by God and leading to God—that the soul enjoys with the priests for whom she or he prays (even if they don't have a particular regular interaction with them). It is the Holy Spirit that inspires such a work and that sustains a soul in such intense and selfless love, and so along with the suffering one can certainly expect to experience (albeit in a divine way, which is not always a human way) the Gifts and Fruits of the Holy Spirit including Joy, Peace, Charity, Fruitfulness, Strength, Courage, Long-suffering, Generosity, Patience, Kindness, Modesty/Chastity, Love, Hope, Faith, Wisdom, Knowledge, Understanding, Right Judgement, Piety, Fear of the Lord, Gentleness, Meekness, Humility, and Purity. As one is an instrument of the Fire of the Divine Love of God for priests (through prayer, suffering and service), she or he themselves will be purified and transformed to be more and more like Our Lady who stood one with Jesus faithful under His Cross.

Chapter 7

Examples of the Saints

I could not conclude a book on the spirituality of praying for priests without a chapter pointing to the example of the saints who have gone before us. Many were called to give their lives to serve, pray for, and suffer for priests. And many saints were the recipients of such prayerful offering. Many saints were shining examples of holy priests themselves.

The first question to touch upon here is the question of how one is called to pray for priests. And my answer would be: valiantly; with bold humility; with courageous trust. There are so many women in the Bible who encompass this sort of prayer, and although they were not always praying specifically for priests in what was recorded of them, I often take them as an example for my own prayer for priests. Praying for priests is entering into spiritual battle and one needs manly courage to face the enemy with peaceful trust that never wavers from its confidence in the Love and Care of God to answer.

Judith

The first person who reminds me of this sort of prayer is Judith. Her prayer is described thus:

> *"Judith threw herself down prostrate, with ashes strewn upon her head, and wearing nothing over her sackcloth. While the incense was being offered in the temple of God in Jerusalem that evening, Judith prayed to the Lord with a loud voice:*
>
> *'It is you who were the author of those events and of what preceded and followed them. The present and the future you have also planned. Whatever you devise comes into being. The things you decide come forward and say, 'Here we are!' All your ways are in readiness, and your judgment is made with foreknowledge.*
>
> *Here are the Assyrians, a vast force, priding themselves on horse and chariot, boasting of the power of their infantry, trusting in shield and spear, bow and sling.*
>
> *They do not know that you are the Lord who crushes wars; Lord is your name.*
>
> *Shatter their strength in your might, and crush their force in your wrath. For they have resolved to profane your sanctuary, to defile the tent where your glorious name resides, and to break off the*

horns of your altar with the sword. See their pride, and send forth your fury upon their heads. Give me, a widow, a strong hand to execute my plan. By the deceit of my lips, strike down slave together with ruler, and ruler together with attendant. Crush their arrogance by the hand of a female.

Your strength is not in numbers, nor does your might depend upon the powerful. You are God of the lowly, helper of those of little account, supporter of the weak, protector of those in despair, savior of those without hope.'" (Judith 9:1; 5-11)

Ester

Another woman who took the burden of the entire Jewish people upon her shoulders and interceded for them before the Lord was Ester:

"Queen Esther, seized with mortal anguish, fled to the Lord for refuge.

Taking off her splendid garments, she put on garments of distress and mourning. In place of her precious ointments she covered her head with dung and ashes. She afflicted her body severely and in place of her festive adornments, her tangled hair covered her.

Then she prayed to the Lord, the God of Israel, saying: "My Lord, you alone are our King. Help me, who am alone and have no help but you, for I am taking my life in my hand. From birth, I have heard among my people that you, Lord, chose Israel from among all nations, and our ancestors from among all their forebears, as a lasting inheritance, and that you fulfilled all your promises to them. But now we have sinned in your sight, and you have delivered us into the hands of our enemies, because we worshiped their gods. You are just, O Lord. But now they are not satisfied with our bitter servitude, but have sworn an oath to their idols to do away with the decree you have pronounced, to destroy your inheritance, to close the mouths of those who praise you, to extinguish the glory of your house and your altar, to open the mouths of the nations to acclaim their worthless gods, and to extol a mortal king forever.

"Lord, do not relinquish your scepter to those who are nothing. Do not let our foes gloat over our ruin, but turn their own counsel against them and make an example of the one who began this against us. Be mindful of us, Lord. Make yourself known in the time of our distress and give me courage, King of gods and Ruler of every power. Put in my mouth persuasive words in the presence of the lion, and

turn his heart to hatred for our enemy, so that he and his co-conspirators may perish. Save us by your power, and help me, who am alone and have no one but you, Lord.

"You know all things. You know that I hate the pomp of the lawless, and abhor the bed of the uncircumcised or of any foreigner. You know that I am under constraint, that I abhor the sign of grandeur that rests on my head when I appear in public. I abhor it like a polluted rag, and do not wear it in private. I, your servant, have never eaten at the table of Haman, nor have I graced the banquet of the king or drunk the wine of libations; From the day I was brought here till now, your servant has had no joy except in you, Lord, God of Abraham. O God, whose power is over all, hear the voice of those in despair. Save us from the power of the wicked, and deliver me from my fear." (Ester 4:12-30)

Martha

We see the heroic faith of Martha when her brother died crying out to the Lord:

"When Martha heard that Jesus was coming, she went to meet him; but Mary sat at home. Martha

said to Jesus, "Lord, if you had been here, my brother would not have died. [But] even now I know that whatever you ask of God, God will give you." Jesus said to her, "Your brother will rise." Martha said to him, "I know he will rise, in the resurrection on the last day." Jesus told her, "I am the resurrection and the life; whoever believes in me, even if he dies, will live, and everyone who lives and believes in me will never die. Do you believe this?" She said to him, "Yes, Lord. I have come to believe that you are the Messiah, the Son of God, the one who is coming into the world." (John 11:20-27)

Other saintly souls

We see this powerful type of prayer in Sarah, pouring out her heart to the Lord, in the book of Tobit; In Hanna weeping for a son; In the Syrophenician woman begging for help for her daughter in the Gospel; And in St. Elizabeth praising God and proclaiming the holiness of her little cousin, Mary. We see it powerfully in Mary Magdalene, weeping at the feet of Jesus anointing them with her tears and oil. There are so many different ways for us to pray, and the Lord wants for us to implement them all as we pray on behalf of our priests.

Throughout the course of history, we have seen saints who prayed for priests as part of their mission of fulfilling

God's will. Even in the Gospel, the women who served Jesus, such as Mary and Martha, who helped their brother Lazarus prepare a place for Him in Bethany, and Lydia, who helped the Apostles in Acts, and many others imitated Our Lady's dedication to caring for Her Priest Son and those who followed in His sacerdotal footsteps. The saints continued this work down through the ages in many different ways. Sts. Fabiola and Paula cared for St. Jerome in Bethlehem. St. Dominic Savio prayed for and inspired Don Bosco. St. Clare gave her entire life to pray for St. Francis and his work, and he would visit her from time to time to receive her prayerful advice on matters. When St. John of the Cross was released from prison, he ran to the sisters of St. Teresa of Avila for shelter, healing, and comfort.

There were also saints whose ministry was specifically dedicated to the spiritual maternity of priests. St Thérèse of Lisieux was overjoyed when her mother superior granted her not just one, but TWO priest brothers to uphold through prayer, sacrifice, and letters of correspondence. Catherine of Siena was sent to advise the Pope, as was St. Bridget of Sweden. St. Gemma Gilgani and St. Faustina spent many hours in prayer and suffering so that their spiritual directors would have the grace to guide them— and both of their spiritual fathers reached heroic sanctity. And then there were more modern-day mystics like Bertha Petit and Blessed Conchita from Mexico who were told by

Our Lady many years in advance (like St. Faustina) to pray for the soul of the priest that He would eventually bring to them to guide them. Some of the saints saw the priest in prayer before they ever met him. Conchita from Mexico was called not only to pray for Archbishop Luiz who would eventually guide her soul, and she founded a religious community of priests, and some of her own sons became priests—her entire life was dedicated to helping, forming, and praying for priests to fulfill their ministries and reach authentic holiness.

It would be good to briefly consider here as well the saintly priests who inspired and transformed (or reformed) the priesthood of their day. St. Vincent de Paul worked relentlessly to renew the priesthood. Others formed confraternities where priests would meet to support each other. St. John of the Cross renewed the Carmelite priests. Pope St. John Paul II greatly renewed the priesthood not only by his extensive writing, but also by his shining example of holiness.

As we conclude this chapter, it would be beneficial to recall some of the holiest priests who have lived and ask for their intercession for our own personal spiritual lives and in our work for praying for the holiness of priests. We should ask the help of St. John Vianney, Don Bosco, John Paul II, Vincent de Paul, Anthony Claret, John of the Cross, Dominic, Padre Pio, Charles de Foucauld, all of the Apostles, Matthias, Barnabas, Timothy, Paul, the Doctors of the Church, Popes, Bishops, Cardinals, Maximillian Kolbe, the priest Martyrs, Confessors, Preachers, St. Louis de Montfort, Titus Brandsma, Jan Sarkander, Ignatius of Loyola, Francis Xavier, Ezekiel Morez, Roque de la Santa Cruz, Augustine, Ambrose, Thomas Aquinas, Paul of the Cross, Vincent Strambi and the list could go on and on. Each one lived their priesthood differently—but each one reached the heights of sanctity that the Lord had intended for them, and in this they can be an inspiration and intercessors for each of us.

At the very end, let us not forget to pray and ask the intercession of the priests of the Old Testament who prepared the way for Christ's new priesthood. We ask for the prayers of Aaron and all the Levites who served throughout the ages in Temple. We ask the intercession of Eli and Zachariah. We also ask the prayers of St. Joseph—who lived a radiant priesthood over the Holy Family for many years—guiding, forming, protecting, helping, and loving Jesus, Who is Our Eternal High priest.

Chapter 8

Pope Benedict XVI's Reflections
on Spiritual Maternity

In 2007, Pope Benedict XVI published a document about Eucharistic Adoration for the sanctification of priests and spiritual maternity. It is providential that it was released on December 8, 2007—and that I find myself finishing this book on that very topic and including his document on December 8, 2020. I pray that Our Lady of the Immaculate Conception intercede for us!

I was unaware of Pope Benedict XVI's document until 2014, when a Franciscan priest I was visiting for some counsel about my spiritual life suggested that it would be something that would resonate powerfully with me and how the Lord was leading me. Upon reading the document, I was taken aback by its beauty and simplicity. I was used to Pope Benedict XVI's writing as usually being theological, yet this was more of an inspirational work that simply gathered stories from holy people who have gone before us. The basis of his publishing the document was to encourage people to spend time in Eucharistic Adoration to intercede for priests, and to give examples specifically of women who had given their lives in praying and sacrificing for the holiness of priests. In the introduction of this document, he writes:

> *"...In order to continually maintain a greater awareness of the ontological link between the Eucharist and the Priesthood, and in order to recognize the special maternity of the Blessed Virgin Mary for each Priest, it is our intention to bring about a connection between perpetual Eucharistic adoration for the sanctification of priests and the initiation of a commitment on the part of con-secrated feminine souls —following the typology of the Blessed Virgin Mary, Mother of the Eternal High Priest, and Helper in his work of Redemp-tion—who might wish to spiritually adopt priests in order to help them with their self-offering, prayer, and penance. Adoration always involves an act of reparation for sins. With that in mind, we suggest a particular intention in this regard..."*

He touches specifically on the role of Our Lady, the *"Mother of the Word Incarnate—the one whom Jesus desired to be intimately united with Himself for the salvation of all humanity."* Referring to Our Lady's title, 'Mother of the Church,' he writes:

"...With reference to the Blessed Virgin Mary, the Second Vatican Council expresses itself in these words: "She conceived, brought forth and nourished Christ. She presented Him to the Father in the temple, and was united with Him by compassion as He died on the Cross. In this singular way She cooperated by Her obedience, faith, hope and burning charity in the work of the Savior in giving back supernatural life to souls. Wherefore She is our mother in the order of grace." (LG 61) Without adding or detracting from the singular mediation of Christ Jesus, the Blessed Virgin Mary is acknowledged and invoked in the Church under the titles of Advocate, Helper, Benefactress, and Mediatrix. She is the model of maternal love who must inspire all those who cooperate—through the apostolic mission of the Church—in the regeneration of all humanity (cfr. LG 65). In light of these teachings, which belong to the ecclesiology of the Second Vatican Council, the faithful are called to turn their eyes to Mary—shining example of every virtue —and imitate Her as the first disciple. It is She to whom every other disciple was entrusted by Christ as She stood at the foot of the cross (cfr. Jn

19:25-27). By becoming Her children, we learn the true meaning of life in Christ. Thereby—and precisely because of the place occupied and the role served by the Most Blessed Virgin in salvation history—we intend in a very particular way to entrust all priests to Mary, the Mother of the High and Eternal Priest, bringing about in the Church a movement of prayer, placing 24 hour continuous Eucharistic adoration at the center, so that a prayer of adoration, thanksgiving, praise, petition, and reparation, will be raised to God, incessantly and from every corner of the earth, with the primary intention of awakening a sufficient number of holy vocations to the priestly state and, at the same time, spiritually uniting with a certain spiritual maternity—at the level of the Mystical Body—all those who have already been called to the ministerial priesthood and are ontologically conformed to the one High and Eternal Priest. This movement will offer better service to Christ and his brothers —those who are at once "inside" the Church and also "at the forefront" of the Church, standing in Christ's stead and representing Him, as head, shepherd and spouse of the Church (cf. Pastores Dabo Vobis 16)."

Pope Benedict XVI then requested that this inspiration of praying for priests—taken from the example of Our Lady's relationship with Jesus, the Eternal High Priest—be promoted within the Church, specifically in regards to Eucharistic Holy Hours offered for priests. He adds:

"We are asking, therefore, all diocesan Ordinaries who apprehend in a particular way the specificity and irreplaceability of the ordained ministry in the life of the Church, together with the urgency of a common action in support of the ministerial priesthood, to take an active role and promote—in the different portions of the People of God entrusted to them—true and proper cenacles in which clerics, religious and lay people— united among themselves in the spirit of true communion—may devote themselves to prayer, in the form of continuous Eucharistic adoration in a spirit of genuine and authentic reparation and purification."

A Great Need for Spiritual Maternity in the Church

In a meeting with the priests and deacons in Freising, Germany on September 14, 2006, Pope Benedict XVI said:

"Pray the Lord of the harvest to send out laborers." *This means that the harvest is ready, but God wishes to enlist helpers to bring it into the*

storehouse. God needs them. He needs people to say: Yes, I am ready to become your harvest laborer; I am ready to offer help so that this harvest which is ripening in people's hearts may truly be brought into the storehouses of eternity and become an enduring, divine communion of joy and love. "Pray the Lord of the harvest" also means that we cannot simply "produce" vocations; they must come from God. Unlike other professions, we cannot simply recruit people by using the right kind of publicity or the correct type of strategy. The call which comes from the heart of God must always find its way into the heart of man. And yet, precisely so that it may reach into hearts, our cooperation is needed. To pray the Lord of the harvest means above all to ask him for this, to stir his heart and say: "Please do this! Rouse laborers! Enkindle in them enthusiasm and joy for the Gospel! Make them understand that this is a treasure greater than any other, and that whoever has discovered it, must hand it on!" We stir the heart of God. But our prayer to God does not consist of words alone; the words must lead to action so that from our praying heart a spark of our joy in God and in the Gospel may arise, enkindling in the hearts of others a readiness to say "yes." As people of prayer, filled with his light, we reach out to others and bring them into our prayer and into the presence of God, who will not fail to do his part. In this sense we must continue to pray the Lord of the harvest, to stir his heart, and together with God touch the hearts of others through our prayer. And he, according to his purpose, will bring to maturity their "yes," their readiness to respond; the constancy, in other words, through all this world's perplexity, through the heat of the day and the darkness of the night, to persevere faithfully in his service. Hence they will know that their efforts, however arduous, are noble and worthwhile because they lead to what is essential, they ensure that people receive what they hope for: God's light and God's love."

In regard to the spiritual motherhood of priests, Pope Benedict recognized that *"The vocation to be a spiritual mother for priests is largely unknown, scarcely understood and, consequently, rarely lived, notwithstanding its fundamental importance. It is a vocation that is frequently hidden, invisible to the naked eye, but meant to transmit spiritual life."* Pope John Paul II was so convinced of the importance of having women dedicating their lives to the fruitfulness of the priestly ministry that he established a cloistered convent *in the Vatican* where nuns would pray for the intentions of the Holy Father. He said once that *'behind every good priest, there is a Mother.'* In this, he was referring not only to the Blessed Mother whose intercession is responsible for the fruitfulness of priestly vocations, but also to the physical and spiritual mothers who formed and continue to uphold (through their prayers and sacrifices) the lives of priests. Pope John Paul, II says,

"Behind this mission (of priesthood) there is the vocation received from God, but there is also hidden the great love of our mothers, just as behind the sacrifice of Christ in the Upper Room there was hidden the ineffable love of his mother. O how truly and yet how discretely is motherhood and thus womanhood present in the Sacrament of Holy Orders!"[6]

Pope Benedict XVI expanded this thought writing:

"Independent of age or social status, any woman can become a mother for priests. This type of motherhood is not only for mothers of families, but is just as possible for an unmarried girl, a widow, or for someone who is ill. It is especially pertinent for missionaries and religious sisters who have given their lives entirely to God for the sanctification of others. John Paul II even thanked a child for her motherly help: "I also express

---

[6] Pope John Paul II, Genius of Woman (Washington, D.C.: United States Catholic Conference, Inc., 1997), p. 66.

my gratitude to Bl. Jacinta for the sacrifices and prayers offered for the Holy Father, whom she saw suffering greatly." (13 May 2000) Every priest has a birth mother, and often she is a spiritual mother for her children as well. For example, Giuseppe Sarto, the future Pope Pius X, visited his 70-year-old mother after being ordained a bishop. She kissed her son's ring and, suddenly pensive, pointed out her own simple silver wedding band saying, "Yes, Giuseppe, you would not be wearing that ring if I had not first worn mine." Pope St. Pius X rightfully confirms his experience that, "Every vocation to the priesthood comes from the heart of God, but it goes through the heart of a mother!""

St. Augustine and St. Monica

The first example that is given by Pope Benedict XVI is of St. Augustine, who, speaking of his mother, said: *"I have my mother to thank for what I have become and the way that I got there!"* St. Augustine had been caught up in non-Christian philosophy and a life of grave sin. His mother, St. Monica, prayed (and wept) for many years for his conversion. One day she approached St. Ambrose begging him to speak to her son and try to convert him. Bishop St. Ambrose responded to St. Monica with a prophesy and a promise saying, *"Woman, the child of so many tears shall never perish."* Sure enough, St. Augustine did eventually convert and not only became a saint, but a holy Bishop and Doctor of the Church! In his ***Confessions,*** St. Augustine referred to his mother Monica's tears and prayer as the cause of his receiving such great graces (of conversion) from the Lord. He wrote,

> *"For love of me, she cried more tears than a mother would over the bodily death of her son. Nine years passed in which I wallowed in the slime of that deep pit and the darkness of falsehood. Yet that pious widow desisted not all the hours of her supplications, to bewail my case unto Thee where her prayers entered into Thy presence."*

Later on, he wrote:

> *My holy mother never abandoned me. She brought me forth in her flesh, that I might be born to this temporal light, and in her heart, that I might be born to life eternal."*

In light of this, we can see the special power and efficacy before God of a motherly heart's supplication for her child's soul (whether it be her physical or spiritual child).

A Cardinal's Dream Nicholas Cardinal of Cusa (1401-1464)

Nicholas Cardinal of Cusa, Bishop of Brixen, was a great Church politician, reputable Papal legate and reformer of spiritual life for the clergy and the faithful of the 15th century. He also was a man of silence and contemplation. He was deeply moved once by a dream about the power of spiritual maternity for priests and all souls, for that matter. The story is thus:

"...(In his dream), Nicholas and his guide entered a small, ancient church decorated with mosaics and frescoes from the early centuries, and there the Cardinal saw an amazing sight. More than a thousand nuns were praying in the little church. Despite the limited space, they all fit due to their slender and composed nature. The sisters were praying, but in a way that the Cardinal had never seen. They were not kneeling but standing; their gaze was not cast off into the distance but rather fixed on something nearby which he could not see. They stood with open arms, palms facing upwards in a gesture of offering. Surprisingly, in their poor, thin hands they carried men and women, emperors and kings, cities and countries. Sometimes there were several pairs of hands joined together holding

a city. A country, recognizable by its national flag, was supported by a whole wall of arms, and yet even then there was an air of silence and isolation around each one of them in prayer. Most of the nuns, however, carried one individual in their hands. In the hands of a thin, young, almost child-like nun, Nicholas saw the Pope. You could see how heavy this load was for her, but her face was radiating a joyful gleam. Standing in the hands of one of the older sisters he saw himself, Nicholas of Cusa, Bishop of Brixen, and Cardinal of the Roman Church. He saw the wrinkles of his age; he saw the blemishes of his soul and his life in all their clarity. He looked with stunned and surprised eyes, but his fright was soon mixed with an unspeakable bliss. His guide whispered, "Now you see how sinners are sustained and carried and, in spite of their sins, have not given up loving God." "What about those who do not love anymore?" the Cardinal asked. Suddenly, he was in the crypt of the church with his guide, where once again, more than a thousand nuns were praying. Whereas the former ones were carried in the nuns' hands, here in the crypt, they were carried in their hearts. They were exceptionally serious because the fate of 13 eternal souls was at hand. "So you see, Your Eminence," said the guide, "that also those who have given up loving are still carried. It happens occasionally that they become warm again through the ardent hearts which are being consumed for them—occasionally, but not always. Sometimes, in the hour of their death, they are taken from these saving hands into the hands of the Divine Judge, and they must also answer for the sacrifice that has been made for them. Every sacrifice bears fruit. However, when the fruit offered to somebody is not picked, the fruit of corruption ripens." The Cardinal was captivated by the women who had made an offering of their lives. He always knew they existed, but he saw now, clearer than ever, their importance for the Church, for the world, for nations and for every individual. Only now was it so surprisingly clear. He bowed deeply before these martyrs of love."

The Example of Eliza Vaughan

Eliza Vaughan was an Englishwoman—a convert from a strong Protestant family—and was a particularly encouraging example of a mother imbued with a priestly spirit who frequently prayed for vocations. After marrying her Catholic husband and converting to Catholicism, Eliza grew in virtue and was a marvelous example of a saintly wife and mother.

"This remarkable woman made a habit of praying for an hour each day before the Blessed Sacrament in the house chapel at Courtfield. She prayed to God for a large family and for many religious vocations among her children. And her prayers were answered! She bore 14 children, and died shortly after the birth of the last child, John, in 1853. Of the 13 children that lived, six of her eight boys became priests: two priests in religious orders, one diocesan priest, a bishop, an archbishop and a cardinal. From the five daughters, four became nuns in religious orders. What a blessing for the family, and what an impact on all of England!"

Christ Entrusts the Renewal of the Priesthood to Women

One example of Jesus calling a woman to follow in the footsteps of His Mother as a spiritual mother of priests was Blessed Maria Deluil Martiny (1841-1884). She once said,

"To offer yourself for souls is beautiful and great... but to offer yourself for the souls of priests is so beautiful, so great, that you would have to have a thousand lives and offer your heart a thousand times... I would gladly give my life if only Christ could find in priests what he is expecting from

them. I would gladly give it even if just one of them could perfectly realize God's divine plan for him!"

She did, in fact, seal her priestly motherhood with the blood of martyrdom at age 43. Her last words were, *"This is for the work, for the Priest Work!"*

Venerable Louise Margaret Claret de la Touche (1868-1915) is another example of a woman called to an apostolate for the renewal of the priesthood.

"The Lord appeared to her on 5 June 1902, while she was in adoration: "Praying to him for our little novitiate, I asked him to give me some souls I might form for him. He replied: 'I will give you the souls of men.' Being profoundly astonished by these words, the sense of which I did not understand, I remained silent...until Jesus said: 'I will give you the souls of priests.' Still more astonished I asked him: 'My Jesus how will you do that?' ...Then he showed me that he has a special work to do, which is to enkindle the fire of love again in the world, and that he wishes to make use of his priests to accomplish it." "He said to me: 'Nineteen centuries ago, twelve men changed the world; they were not merely men, but they were priests. Now, once more twelve priests could change the world...but they must be holy.'" Subsequently, the Lord let Louise Margaret see the outcome of the

Work. "It is a special union of priests, a Work, which encompasses the whole world. ... Priests who will form part of this work will undertake, among other things, to preach Infinite Love and mercy, but first his heart must be penetrated by Jesus and enlightened by his spirit of love. They must be united among themselves, having but one heart and one soul, and never impeding one another in their activities." Louise Margaret wrote so impressively about the priesthood in her book "The Sacred Heart and the Priesthood", that priests believed the anonymous writer to be a fellow priest. A Jesuit even exclaimed, "I do not know who wrote this book, but one thing I do know, it is not the work of a woman!"

We can see the power of spiritual maternity of priesthoods not only as fruitful in families and religious houses, but also for entire cities. The little village of Lu, in northern Italy, is located in a rural area 90 kilometres east of Turin. In 1881, the mothers of this village made a decision that would impact all of Italy (and the world.) Many of these mothers had a burning desire in their hearts for one of their sons to become a priest or a daughter to be a religious. And so,

"...under the direction of their parish priest, Msgr. Alessandro Canora, they gathered every Tuesday for adoration of the Blessed Sacrament, asking the Lord for vocations. They received Holy Communion on the first Sunday of every month with the same intention. After Mass, all the mothers prayed a particular prayer together imploring for vocations to the priesthood. Through the trusting prayer of these mothers and the openness of the other parents, an atmosphere of deep joy and Christian piety developed in the families, making it much easier for the children to recognize their vocations... No one expected that God would hear the prayers of these mothers in such a dramatic way. From the tiny village of Lu came 323 vocations: 152 priests (diocesan and religious), and 171 nuns belonging to 41 different congregations. As many as three or four vocations came from some of the families. The most famous example is the Rinaldi family, from whom God called seven children. Two daughters became Salesian sisters, both of whom were sent to San Domingo as missionaries. Five sons became priests, all joining the Salesians. The most well-known of the Rinaldi brothers is Blessed Philip Rinaldi, who became the third successor of St. John Bosco as Superior General of the Salesians. Pope John Paul II beatified him on 29 April 1990. In

fact, many of the vocations from this small town became Salesians. It is certainly not a coincidence, since St. John Bosco visited Lu four times during his life. The saint attended the first Mass of his spiritual son, Fr. Philip Rinaldi in this village where he was born."

The prayer that the mothers of Lu prayed was short, simple, and deep:

"O God, grant that one of my sons may become a priest! I myself want to live as a good Christian and want to guide my children always to do what is right, so that I may receive the grace, O God, to be allowed to give you a holy priest! Amen."

Two Souls Consecrated Especially to Pray for Priests

Pope Benedict XVI mentions in his document two extraordinary souls who were called to pray and suffer specifically for the souls of priests who were trapped in sin. He writes:

"Blessed Alessandrina da Costa (1904-1955)

A story from the life of Alexandrina da Costa, beatified on 25 April 2004, reveals the transforming power and visible effects of the sacrifice made by a sick and forgotten girl. In 1941, Alexandrina wrote to her spiritual director, Fr. Mariano Pinho, telling him that Jesus told her, "My daughter, a priest living in Lisbon is close to being lost forever; he offends me terribly. Call your spiritual director and ask his permission that I may have you suffer in a special way for this soul." Once Alexandrina had received permission from her spiritual director, she suffered greatly. She felt the severity of the priest's errors, how he wanted to know nothing about God and was close to self-damnation. She even heard the priest's full name. Poor Alexandrina experienced the hellish state of this priest's soul and prayed urgently, "Not to hell, no! I offer myself as a sacrifice for him, as long as you want." Fr. Pinho inquired of the Cardinal of Lisbon whether one of the priests of his diocese was of particular concern. The Cardinal openly confirmed that he was, in fact, very worried about one of his priests, and when he mentioned the name of the priest, it was the same one that Jesus had spoken to Alexandrina. Some months later, a friend of Fr. Pinho, Fr. David Novais, recounted to him an unusual incident. Fr. David had just held a retreat in Fatima where attended a modest gentleman whose exemplary behavior made him pleasantly attractive to all the participants. On the last night of the retreat, this man suddenly had a heart attack. He asked to see a priest, to whom he confessed and received Holy Communion. Shortly thereafter he died, fully reconciled with God. It turned out that this man was actually a priest—the very priest for whom Alexandrina had suffered so greatly.

Servant of God Consolata Betrone (1903-1946)

The sacrifices and prayers of a spiritual mother for priests benefit especially those who have strayed or abandoned their vocations. Jesus has called count-less women in his Church to this vocation of prayer, such as Sister Consolata Betrone, a Capuchin nun from Turin. Jesus said to her, "Your life-long task is for your brothers. Consolata, you too, shall be a good shepherdess and go in search of your brothers and bring them back to me." Consolata offered everything for "her brother" priests and others consecrated to God who were in spiritual need. While working in the kitchen, she prayed continuously in her heart, "Jesus, Mary, I love you, save souls!" She consciously made every little service and duty into a sacrifice. Jesus said in this regard, "Your duties may be insignificant, but because you bring them to me with such love, I give them *immeasurable value and shower them on the discontented brothers as grace for conversion."* Very grave and difficult cases were often entrusted to the prayers of the convent. Consolata would take the corresponding suffering upon herself. For weeks or months on end she sometimes endured dryness of spirit, abandonment, meaninglessness, inner darkness, loneliness, doubt, and the sinful state of the priests. She once wrote to her spiritual director during these struggles, "How much the brothers cost me!" Yet Jesus made her a magnificent promise, "Consolata, it is not only one brother that you will lead back to God, but all of them. I promise you, you will give me the brothers, one after another." And so it was! She brought back all of the priests entrusted to her to a fulfilling priesthood. There are recorded testimonies of many of these cases."*

Chosen Souls called to suffer for the Priests who would be their Spiritual Guides

Twenty years ago, while I was still studying at the University of Notre Dame, I first heard from my spiritual director at the time about a few chosen souls asked by Jesus to suffer and pray for the priests whom He would bring to them eventually to guide their souls. This was similar to what happened with St. Faustina, as she saw a vision of Fr. Sopocko before she ever met him. At that time, I was inspired to offer my life to pray and suffer for specific priestly souls—and specifically for the one/s who would be asked by Jesus someday to help guide me. Although not all souls will receive an actual revelation as to who or how the Lord will bring a priest to help them on their spiritual path, it is a good practice for ALL SOULS to pray for those priests who have impacted (or will impact) their own personal spiritual lives. This idea was first presented to me in the lives of Berthe Petit (1870-1943) from Belgium, and Venerable Conchita of Mexico (1862-1937).

*"**Berthe Petit**, a great mystic and expiatory soul from Belgium, has remained relatively unknown to this day. Jesus clearly indicated the priest for whom she was to give up her own plans, and providence even let them meet. As a 15-year-old girl, Berthe began praying at every Holy Mass for the celebrant, "My Jesus, do not allow your priests to displease you!" When she was 17 years old, her parents lost everything they had in a failed business venture. On 8 December 1888, Berthe's confessor explained to her that her vocation was not to enter a convent but to stay at home and care for her parents. Although she accepted this sacrifice with a heavy heart, Berthe asked Our Lady to intercede that Jesus might call a*

zealous and holy priest in the place of her religious vocation. "You will certainly be heard!" assured her confessor. She could not have known what would take place just 16 days later: A 22-year-old lawyer, Dr. Louis Decorsant, was praying before a statue of the Sorrowful Mother. Unexpectedly, he had an inner certainty that it was not his vocation to take the girl he loved to be his wife and to establish himself as a notary. He understood very clearly that God was calling him to be a priest. The call was so clear and urgent that he did not hesitate to give up everything. Upon finishing his studies and his doctorate in Rome, he was ordained to the priesthood in Paris in 1893. At the time, Berthe was 22 years old. That same year, the newly ordained, 27- year-old priest celebrated Christmas Midnight Mass in a church outside Paris. At the exact moment Berthe was participating at Midnight Mass in another church, and solemnly promised the Lord, "Jesus, I will be a sacrifice for the priests, for all priests, but especially for the priest of my life." During exposition of the Blessed Sacrament, the young woman suddenly saw Jesus hanging on a large cross and Mary and John standing beneath it. Then she heard the words, "Your offer has been accepted, your prayer heard. Behold your priest... you will be able to meet him one day." And Berthe saw that John's features resembled a priest, but one she did not know. This priest was none other than Fr. Decorsant whom she would recognize at their first encounter—some 15 years later in 1908.

Berthe made a pilgrimage to Lourdes where the Blessed Virgin confirmed, "Now you will see the priest whom you asked God for 20 years ago; you will meet him soon." That same year, she made another trip by train to Lourdes, this time with a friend of hers. A priest got on at the station in Paris trying to find a place for a sick woman. It was Fr. Decorsant. His features were those which Berthe had seen on St. John's face 15 years earlier. She had prayed frequently and offered all of her physical suffering for him. After a couple of friendly words, he left the compartment. Exactly one month later, Fr. Decorsant also made a pilgrimage to Lourdes because he wanted to entrust the future of his priesthood to Our Lady. With suitcases in hand, he met Berthe and her friend. Recognizing the two women, he invited them to Holy Mass. When Fr. Decorsant elevated the Host, Jesus interiorly said to Berthe, "This is the priest for whom I accepted your sacrifice." After the Holy Mass, Berthe was surprised to see that the "priest of her life," as she called him from then on, was staying in the same hotel as they were. Shortly thereafter, Berthe was able to speak to him about her interior life and another mission that was entrusted to her—the promulgation of the consecration to the Immaculate and Sorrowful Heart of Mary. Fr. Decorsant felt that this precious soul had been entrusted to him by God. He accepted a position in Belgium and became a holy spiritual director for Berthe Petit as well as an untiring support for the realization of her mission. Theologically sound, he was the ideal person to maintain a correspondence between Berthe and the hierarchy of the Church in Rome. For the 24 years until his death, he accompanied Berthe Petit in her expiatory vocation; she was often very sick and suffered especially for priests who had left the priesthood.

Venerable Conchita of Mexico

Maria Conception Cabrera de Armida ("Conchita") was a wife and mother with children. Over the course of many years, Jesus prepared her to live a life of spiritual motherhood for priests. In the future, she will be of great importance for the universal Church. Jesus once explained to Conchita, "There are souls, who through ordination receive a priestly anointing. However, there are ... also priestly souls who do not have the dignity or the ordination of a priest, yet have a priestly mission.

They offer themselves united to me... these souls help the Church in a very powerful spiritual way. ... You will be the mother of a great number of spiritual children, yet they will cost your heart the death of a thousand martyrs. "Bring yourself as an offering for the priests. Unite your offering with my offering, to obtain graces for them." ... "I want to come again into this world. ... in my priests. I want to renew the world by revealing myself through the priests. I want to give my Church a powerful impulse in which I will pour out the Holy Spirit over my priests like a new Pentecost. "The Church and the world need a new Pentecost, a priestly Pentecost, an interior Pentecost." As a young girl, Conchita once prayed before the Blessed Sacrament, "Lord, I feel so incapable of loving you; therefore, I want to marry. Give me many children so that they can love you more than I." She had a very happy marriage, and gave birth to nine children—two girls and seven boys, each of whom she consecrated to Our Lady, "I give them entirely to you as your children. You know that I am not capable of raising them. I understand too little of what it means to be a mother. But you...you know it." She endured the death of four of her children, each dying a holy death.

Naturally, Conchita's spiritual motherhood was very apparent in one of her sons who became a priest. She wrote about him, 25 "Manuel was born in the same hour that Fr. José Camacho died. Upon hearing the news, I prayed to God that my son could replace him at the altar. ... When little Manuel began to talk, we prayed together for the great grace of a vocation to the priesthood. ... On the day of his First Holy Communion and on all the major solemnities, he renewed this prayer. ... At the age of 17, he joined the Society of Jesus." Her third child, Manuel was born in 1889. While living in Spain, he wrote to his mother about his decision to become a priest. She wrote back to him, *"Give yourself to the Lord with all your heart, and do not hold anything back! Forget about creatures and forget especially about yourself! I cannot imagine someone consecrated to God who is not a saint. One cannot give only half of oneself to God. Be generous with him!"*

In 1914, she met Manuel in Spain for the last time, because he never returned to Mexico. He wrote in a letter to her, *"My dear little mother, you have shown me the way. Fortunately, I have heard from your lips since my earliest years the challenging and saving teaching of the Cross. Now I want to put it into practice."* His mother felt the pain of separation, *"I took your letter to the tabernacle and told the Lord that I accept this sacrifice with my whole soul. The next day I was carrying your letter close to my heart when I received Holy Communion and, in this way, renewed my total offering to the Lord." "Mother, teach me how to be a priest!" On 23 July 1922, one week before his ordination to the priesthood, the 33-year-old Manuel asked Conchita in a letter, "Mother, teach me how to be a priest! Tell me about the immeasurable joy of being able to celebrate Holy Mass. I put everything back into your hands, just as when you held me to your chest as a very small child, teaching me the beautiful names of Jesus and Mary and introducing me to this mystery. I really feel like an infant asking for your light, your prayer and your sacrifice. ... As soon as I am a priest, I will send you my blessing, and then I will receive yours on my knees." On 31 July 1922, as Manuel was being ordained to the priesthood in Barcelona, Conchita woke up in the middle of the night so that she could participate spiritually in his ordination. She was overcome by the awareness, "I am the mother of a priest! ... I can only cry and give thanks! I invite all of heaven to give thanks in my place because I am incapable of doing it, I who am so wretched." Ten years later, she wrote to her son, "I cannot imagine a priest who is not Jesus, even less so in the Society of Jesus. I pray that your transformation into Christ, through celebrating Holy Mass, may help you to become Jesus day and night." (17 May 1932) "What would we do without the Cross? Life would be unbearable without pain; it unites, sanctifies, purifies and attains grace." (10 June 1932) Fr. Manuel died a holy death in 1955 at the age of 66.*

The Lord enlightened Conchita regarding her apostolate, "I will entrust to you a different martyrdom: you will suffer what the priests undertake against me. You will experience and offer up their infidelity and wretchedness." This spiritual motherhood for the sanctification of priests and the Church consumed her completely. Conchita died in 1937 at the age of 75."

Spiritual Maternity of Priests through Prayer, Sacrifices and Letters

Some special souls have been chosen by God to be a spiritual encouragement for priests not only through prayer and sacrifice, but also through concrete friendship and an exchange of letters. Many saints have upheld their spiritual brothers in this way (and I named a few in the previous chapters), but an example that Pope Benedict XVI chose to expand on was the mission of St. Therese of Lisieux to her 'little priest brothers.' He writes:

"St. Therese of Lisieux (1873-1897) On a pilgrimage to Rome, when she was only 14 years old, Therese came to understand her vocation to be a spiritual mother for priests. In her autobiography she describes that after meeting many holy priests

on her trip to Italy, she understood their weaknesses and fraility in spite of their sublime dignity. "If holy priests...show in their conduct their extreme need for prayers, what is to be said of those who are tepid?" (A 157) In one of her letters she encouraged her sister Céline, "Let us live for souls, let us be apostles, let us save especially the souls of priests. ... Let us pray, let us suffer for them, and, on the last day, Jesus will be grateful." (LT 94) In the life of Therese, Doctor of the Church, there is a moving episode which highlights her zeal for souls, especially missionaries. While she was very ill and had great difficulty walking, the nurse advised her to take a little walk in the garden for a quarter of an hour each day. She obeyed faithfully, although she did not find it effective. On one occasion, the sister accompanying her noticed how painful it was for her to walk and remarked "You would do better to rest; this walking can do you no good under such conditions. You're exhausting yourself." The saint responded, "Well, I am walking for a missionary. I think that over there, far away, one of them is perhaps exhausted in his apostolic endeavors, and, to lessen his fatigue, I offer mine to God." God gave a clear sign of accepting Therese's desire to offer her life for priests when the mother superior gave her the name of two seminarians who had asked for spiritual support from a Carmelite nun. The future Abbot Maurice Bellière was one of them. Just a few days after the death of Therese, he received the habit of the "White Fathers" as a priest and missionary. Adolphe Roulland was the other seminarian whom she accompanied through her prayers and sacrifices until his ordination."

William Emmanuel Ketteler (1811-1877) "My Priesthood and a Stranger"

Pope Benedict offers another brilliant example of God calling someone to prayerfully uphold another in their priesthood, even without either recipient knowing about it for many years. The story of Bishop Ketteler is one such story and is also presented as an inspiration in this document:

"Each of us owes gratitude for our lives and our vocations to the prayers and sacrifices of others. One of the leading figures of the German episcopacy of the 19th century, and among the founders of Catholic sociology, Bishop Ketteler owed his gratitude to a simple nun, the least and poorest lay sister of her convent. In 1869, a German diocesan bishop was sitting together with his guest, Bishop Ketteler from Mainz. During the course of

their conversation, the diocesan bishop brought up his guest's extremely blessed apostolate. Bishop Ketteler explained to his host, "I owe thanks for everything that I have accomplished with God's help, to the prayer and sacrifice of someone I do not even know. I can only say that I know somebody has offered his or her whole life to our loving God for me, and I have this sacrifice to thank that I even became a priest."

He continued, "Originally, I wasn't planning on becoming a priest. I had already finished my law degree and thought only about finding an important place in the world to begin acquiring honor, prestige and wealth. An extraordinary experience held me back and directed my life down a different path. "One evening I was alone in my room, considering my future plans of fame and fortune, when something happened which I cannot explain. Was I awake or asleep? Did I really see it or was it just a dream? One thing I do know, it brought about a change in my life.

I saw Jesus very clearly and distinctly standing over me in a radiant cloud, showing me his Sacred Heart. A nun was kneeling before him, her hands raised up in prayer. From his mouth, I heard the words, 'She prays unremittingly for you!' "I distinctly saw the appearance of the sister, and her traits made such an impression on me that she has remained in my memory to this day. She seemed to be quite an ordinary lay sister. Her clothing was very poor and rough. Her hands were red and calloused from hard work. Whatever it was, a dream or not, it was extraordinary. It shook me to the depths of my being so that from that moment on, I decided to consecrate myself to God in the service of the priesthood. "I withdrew to a monastery for a retreat, and I talked about everything with my confessor. Then, at the age of 30, I began studying theology. You know the rest of the story. So, if you think that I have done something admirable, now you know who really deserves the credit—a religious sister who prayed for me, maybe without even knowing who I was. I am convinced, I was prayed for and I will continue to be prayed for in secret and that without these prayers, I could never have reached the goal that God has destined for me."

"Do you have any idea of the whereabouts or the identity of who has prayed for you?" asked the diocesan bishop. "No, I can only ask God each day that, while she is still on earth, he bless and repay her a thousand-fold for what she has done for me."

The next day, Bishop Ketteler visited a convent of sisters in a nearby city and celebrated Holy Mass in their chapel. He was distributing Holy Communion to the last row of sisters when one of them suddenly caught his eye. His face grew pale, and he stood there, motionless. Finally regaining his composure, he gave Holy Communion to the sister who was kneeling in recollection unaware of his hesitation. He then concluded the liturgy. The bishop who had invited him the previous day came and joined him at the convent for breakfast. When they had finished, Bishop Ketteler asked the Mother Superior to present to him all the sisters in the house. Before long she had gathered all the sisters together, and both bishops went to meet them. Bishop Ketteler greeted them, but it was apparent that he did not find the one he was looking for. He quietly asked the Mother Superior, "Are all the sisters really here?" She looked over the group of sisters and then said, "Your Excellency, I called them all, but, in fact, one of them is not here." "Why didn't she come?" "She works in the barn," answered the superior, "and in such a commendable way that, in her enthusiasm, she sometimes forgets other things." "I would like to see that sister," requested the Bishop. A little while later, the sister who had been summoned stepped into the room. Again Bishop Ketteler turned pale, and after a few words to all the sisters, he asked if he could be alone with the sister who had just come in.

"Do you know me?" he asked her. "I have never seen Your Excellency before." "Have you ever prayed for me or offered up a good deed for me?" he wanted to know. "I do not recall that I have ever heard of Your Excellency." The Bishop was silent for a few moments and then he asked, "Do you have a particular devotion that you like?" "The devotion to the Sacred Heart of Jesus," was the response. "You have, it seems, the most difficult task in the convent," he continued. "Oh no, Your Excellency" the sister countered, "but I cannot lie, it is unpleasant for me." "And what do you do when you have such temptations against your work?" "For things that cost me greatly, I grew accustomed to facing them with joy and enthusiasm out of love for God, and then I offer them up for one soul on earth. To whom God chooses to be gracious as a result, I have left completely up to him and I do not want to know.

I also offer up my time of Eucharistic adoration every evening from 8 to 9 for this intention." "Where did you get the idea to offer up all your merits for someone totally unknown to you?" "I learned it while I was still out in the world," she replied. "At school our teacher, the parish priest, taught us how we can pray and offer our merits for our relatives. Besides that, he said that we should pray much for those who are in danger of being lost. Since only God knows who really needs prayer, it is best to put your merits at the disposition of the Sacred Heart of Jesus trusting in his wisdom and omnipotence. That is what I have done," she concluded, "and I always believed that God would find the right soul."

"How old are you?" Ketteler asked. "Thirty-three, Your Excellency," she answered. The Bishop paused a moment. Then he asked her, "When were you born?" The sister stated her day of birth. The Bishop gasped; her birthday was the day of his conversion! Back then he saw her exactly as she was before him now. "And have you any idea whether your prayers and sacrifices have been successful?" he asked her further. "No, Your Excellency." "Don't you want to know?" "Our dear God knows when something good happens, and that is enough," was the simple answer. The Bishop was shaken. "So continue this work in the name of the Lord," he said. The sister knelt down immediately at his feet and asked for his blessing. The Bishop solemnly raised his hands and said with great emotion, "With the power entrusted to me as a bishop, I bless your soul, I bless your hands and their work, I bless your

prayers and sacrifices, your self-renunciation and your obedience. I bless especially your final hour and ask God to assist you with all his consolation."
"Amen," the sister answered calmly, then stood up and left.

The Bishop, profoundly moved, stepped over to the window in order to compose himself. Some time later, he said good-bye to the Mother Superior and returned to the apartment of his bishop friend. He confided to him, "Now I found the one I have to thank for my vocation. It is the lowest and poorest lay sister of that convent. I cannot thank God enough for his mercy because this sister has prayed for me for almost 20 years. On the day she first saw the light of the world, God worked my conversion accepting in advance her future prayers and works. "What a lesson and a reminder for me! Should I become tempted to vanity by a certain amount of success or by my good works, then I can affirm in truth: You have the prayer and sacrifice of a poor maid in a convent stall to thank. And when a small and lowly task appears of little value to me, then I will also remember the fact: what this maid does in humble obedience to God, making a sacrifice by overcoming herself, is so valuable before the Lord Our God that her merits have given rise to a bishop for the Church."

"Lord, Give Us Priests Again!"

I remember during the time that I served as a missionary in Eastern Siberia, reading something about a village in Western Siberia shortly after the Communists had murdered all of the priests. The villagers were so longing for priestly guidance and especially for absolution from their sins that they would often gather at the cemetery around the graves of their murdered priests, confessing their sins aloud and hoping that in God's mercy He would send absolution to them from heaven. Pope Benedict XVI mentions one particular story of a similar light from Russia that ended with the reward of a return of priests to their area. This was primarily because of the prayer and sacrifice of a woman named Anna Stang. She said that after the Communist persecution, *"We were left without pastors!"* Yet, God raised up in her such a priestly heart that through her many years of prayer and sacrifice, priests were led back to her people. Here is her story:

> *"Anna Stang endured great suffering during the Communist persecution, and like many other women in her situation, she offered it up for priests. In her old age, she has become a woman with a priestly spirit.*
>
> *Anna Stang was born in 1909 to a large faithful family living in the German area of the Volga in*

Russia. She began suffering for the faith as a nine-year-old schoolgirl. She writes, "...In 1918, in second grade, we still prayed the Our Father before class. One year later, everything was forbidden and the priest was no longer allowed in the school. People began to laugh at those of us who believed, showing no respect for the priests anymore, and the seminary was destroyed." When she was 11 years old, Anna lost her father and several siblings to a Cholera epidemic. When her mother died six years later, Anna was left to raise her younger brothers and sisters. Not only did they lose their parents, but, "Our priest also died at this time, and many religious were arrested. So we were left without a pastor! That was so difficult. ... In the neighboring parish, the church was still open, but there was no longer a priest there either. The faithful gathered for prayer, but without a priest, the church was very cold. I just used to cry, no longer being able to hold myself together. Earlier, this church had been filled with so much song and prayer! Everything seemed dead to me." Deeply afflicted by this spiritual suffering, Anna prayed from that moment on—especially for priests and missionaries- "Lord, Give Us Priests Again!"

Anna Stang endured great suffering during the Communist persecution, and like many other women in her situation, she offered it up for priests. In her old age, she has become a woman with a priestly spirit. "We were left without pastors!" "Lord, give us another priest, give us Holy Communion! I gladly suffer everything for you, O most Sacred Heart of Jesus!" All the suffering which she endured in the following years, she consciously offered for priests—even when the Communists raided their house in 1938 and arrested her brother and the husband to whom she had been happily married for seven years. Neither of them ever returned.

In 1942, the young widow was deported with her three children to Kazachstan. "It was hard, arriving in the bitter cold of winter, but we lived through it to see spring. In those days I cried a lot, but I also prayed a lot. It was always as if somebody was leading me by the hand. Sometime later, I found some Catholic women in the city of Siryanovsk. We secretly congregated on Sundays and solemnities to sing hymns and pray the Rosary. I prayed so often, 'Mary, our beloved Mother, see how poor we are; send us priests, teachers and pastors again!'"

The persecution subsided somewhat after 1965. "A church was even built in Bishkek (the capital of Kirgizstan), and once a year my friend Veronica and

I went there for Holy Mass. It was a long way, more than 1000 kilometres, but we were so happy to go. We had not seen a priest or a confessional for more than 20 years! The priest there was old and had spent 10 years in prison for his faith. While I was there, somebody lent me a key to the church allowing me to spend a long time in adoration. I never thought that I would be so close to the tabernacle again, and in my joy, I knelt down and kissed it." Before returning home, Anna always received permission to bring Holy Communion back to the Catholics in her city who could not make such a trip. *"With the mandate of the priest, I baptized the children and adults in my city for 30 years; I led couples to the sacrament of marriage and buried the dead until my health no longer permitted it."*

You cannot imagine how thankful Anna was when a missionary priest visited her home for the first time in 1995. She cried for joy and said so movingly, "Jesus the High Priest has come!" At 86 years of age, having prayed for decades for priests and missionaries, she no longer believed she would see them again. Holy Mass was celebrated for the first time in the apartment of this exceptional woman who possessed a true priestly spirit. Out of reverence and joy for the reception of Holy Communion, she ate nothing for the entire day."

Chapter 9

Our Lady (and Her Children) as a Shepherdess of Souls and a Mirror of Jesus Christ, the Eternal High Priest

Mary as a Shepherdess

Our Lady was imbued with the Spirit of Christ through the compenetration (union) of Hearts that they shared to the extent of taking on Her shoulders, into Her hands, and into Her Heart the burdens that Jesus bore, which were the burdens of the 'sheep' entrusted to His care and love. Isaiah 53:4-5 says that *"It was our pain that he bore, our sufferings he endured. We thought of him as stricken, struck down by God and afflicted, But he was pierced for our sins, crushed for our iniquity. He bore the punishment that makes us whole, by his wounds we were healed."* And Mary 'helps' Christ in His suffering by living what He lives in union with Him. We are called to do the same—as we see from the many examples given to us in Pope Benedict XVI's document above. Numerous souls in the history of the

Church have been asked by God to be drawn into the priestly suffering of Christ in order to 'help' Him in His priestly work—with and for His priest sons on earth. And Our Lady is our model in this. It is in virtue of Her relationship with Jesus (and union with His Heart) as the Eternal High Priest that Our Lady has the knowledge of how to care for souls. And it is precisely from His Heart mystically indwelling with Her Own that She receives the strength to carry out Her role as the 'Good Shepherdess' with Him.

Mary is a Shepherdess who spares no pain nor sacrifice to keep Her sheep safe and happy. Jesus does this on the Cross. Mary does this by the Cross in Her Heart—through the powerful sword thrust through Her Love foretold by Simeon in the Presentation in the Temple. *"...And you yourself a sword will pierce so that the thoughts of many hearts may be revealed."* (Luke 2:35) St. Pope John Paul II once said, 'Mary doesn't win Her battle against satan with a sword in Her hand, but with a sword in Her Heart.' We are called to walk the same way as Mary and Jesus by shepherding souls with the Love that They share with our hearts. We are called to shepherd souls by the Love pouring forth from the Cross anchored in our hearts. We are baptized into this—it is not an 'extra grace' for just a few or a luxury; it is a responsibility given to us in virtue of our baptism.

Chapter 4 of *Lumen Gentium* states that the laity *"are by baptism made one body with Christ and are constituted among the People of God; they are in their own way made sharers in the priestly, prophetical, and kingly functions of Christ; and they carry out for their own part the mission of the whole Christian people in the Church and in the world."* (paragraph 31) It goes on to say in Paragraph 34 that:

> *"The supreme and eternal Priest, Christ Jesus, since he wills to continue his witness and service also through the laity, vivifies them in this Spirit and increasingly urges them on to every good and perfect work.*
>
> *For besides intimately linking them to His life and His mission, He also gives them a sharing in His priestly function of offering spiritual worship for the glory of God and the salvation of men. For this reason the laity, dedicated to Christ and anointed by the Holy Spirit, are marvelously called and wonderfully prepared so that ever more abundant fruits of the Spirit may be produced in them. For all their works, prayers and apostolic endeavors, their ordinary married and family life, their daily occupations, their physical and mental relaxation, if carried out in the Spirit, and even the hardships of life, if patiently borne—all these*

become "spiritual sacrifices acceptable to God through Jesus Christ".(199) Together with the offering of the Lord's body, they are most fittingly offered in the celebration of the Eucharist. Thus, as those everywhere who adore in holy activity, the laity consecrate the world itself to God."

The *Catechism of the Catholic Church* also refers to this union of the baptized with the priestly role of Christ in paragraphs 783 and 784. It states:

*"Jesus Christ is the one whom the Father anointed with the Holy Spirit and established as priest, prophet, and king. **The whole People of God participates in these three offices of Christ and bears the responsibilities for mission and service that flow from them.***

On entering the People of God through faith and Baptism, one receives a share in this people's unique, priestly vocation: "Christ the Lord, high priest taken from among men, has made this new people 'a kingdom of priests to God, his Father.' The baptized, by regeneration and the anointing of the Holy Spirit, are consecrated to be a spiritual house and a holy priesthood."

Here we see that the laity (and Our Lady was part of the laity as a common housewife and mother—even if Her spiritual life was extraordinary) are called to partake in Christ's role as Priest. Jesus as the High Priest offers Himself to the Father in expiation for sin. All baptized people who make up the Body of Christ partake in this offering with Him. *"Now you are Christ's body, and individually parts of it."* (1 Cor 12:27) *"Now I rejoice in my sufferings for your sake, and in my flesh I am filling up what is lacking in the afflictions of Christ on behalf of his body, which is the church."* (Col 1:24) *"I urge you therefore, brothers, by the mercies of God, to offer your bodies as a living sacrifice, holy and pleasing to God, your spiritual worship."* (Rom 12:1) It is by virtue of our baptism that our 'prayers, works, joys, sorrows, sufferings, rest, thoughts, and actions' may have salvific meaning for the world when united to Christ in His Sacrifice. Jesus as the High Priest worships the Father—we see in Scripture several times when Jesus cried out *'Father, I praise You! Father, I thank you!'* (Mt 11:25) Our Lady imitates Him in this praying, *"My soul proclaims the greatness of the Lord; my spirit rejoices in God my savior."* (Lk 1:46-47) And we are called to do the same—in union with them.

"Blessed be the God and Father of our Lord Jesus Christ, the Father of compassion and God of all

encouragement, who encourages us in our every affliction, so that we may be able to encourage those who are in any affliction with the encouragement with which we ourselves are encouraged by God. For as Christ's sufferings overflow to us, so through Christ does our encouragement also overflow. If we are afflicted, it is for your encouragement and salvation; if we are encouraged, it is for your encouragement, which enables you to endure the same sufferings that we suffer. Our hope for you is firm, for we know that as you share in the sufferings, you also share in the encouragement." (2 Cor 1:3-7)

"Blessed be the God and Father of our Lord Jesus Christ, who in his great mercy gave us a new birth to a living hope through the resurrection of Jesus Christ from the dead..." (1 Peter 1:3)

"Blessed be the God and Father of our Lord Jesus Christ, who has blessed us in Christ with every spiritual blessing in the heavens, as he chose us in him, before the foundation of the world, to be holy and without blemish before him. In love he destined us for adoption to himself through Jesus Christ, in accord with the favor of his will, for the praise of the

glory of his grace that he granted us in the beloved." (Eph 1:3-6)

We are all called—and even more so especially those who are asked to pray and suffer for priests—to partake in the Priesthood of Jesus Christ by uniting not only our prayer with His Prayer and our worship of the Father with His Worship, but by uniting our entire lives as a sacrifice of love united with Him. Every heartbeat, every footstep, every word, every thought, every action can be offered in a 'priestly' way as a sacrifice of love united to Him (especially as present in the priesthood) for the salvation of the world. It is precisely in living out this call by God that we best are able to pray for, aid, and be a helpmate to priests in con-crete ways. We unite with their priesthood through our union with Christ—and we then help them in shepherding souls as Our Lady (the 'Great Shepherdess') helps Christ with all of us.

Mary as a Mirror

Ordained priests are set aside from the lay faithful in that they live a special union with Christ—because of their ordination they are able to pray and serve *in persona Christi.*

The *Catechism of the Catholic Church* explains in paragraphs 1548 and 1549:

> *In the ecclesial service of the ordained minister, it is Christ himself who is present to his Church as Head of his Body, Shepherd of his flock, high priest of the redemptive sacrifice, Teacher of Truth. This is what the Church means by saying that the priest, by virtue of the sacrament of Holy Orders, acts in persona Christi Capitis.*

> *It is the same priest, Christ Jesus, whose sacred person his minister truly represents. Now the minister, by reason of the sacerdotal consecration which he has received, is truly made like to the high priest and possesses the authority to act in the power and place of the person of Christ himself (virtute ac persona ipsius Christi).*
> *Christ is the source of all priesthood: the priest of the old law was a figure of Christ, and the priest of the new law acts in the person of Christ.*

> *Through the ordained ministry, especially that of bishops and priests, the presence of Christ as head of the Church is made visible in the midst of the community of believers.*[26] *In the beautiful expression of St. Ignatius of Antioch, the bishop*

is typos tou Patros: he is like the living image of God the Father.

Our Lady lived from the Incarnation onward mysteriously in union with Jesus, the Eternal High Priest—not '*in persona Christi'* as the head of the body, but instead as a Helpmate giving life and love to the heart of Christ's body. In this, She is the mirror we should try to reflect in our own ministries of loving, praying for, and serving priests. As I already explained, all of the faithful '*make up what is lacking in the suffering of Christ.'* All are called to be the priest, altar and victim (to make of our bodies an offering to God—"*For we are the aroma of Christ for God among those who are being saved and among those who are perishing"*—2 Cor 2:15 *"So be imitators of God, as beloved children, and live in love, as Christ loved us and handed himself over for us as a sacrificial offering to God for a fragrant aroma… addressing one another [in] psalms and hymns and spiritual songs, singing and playing to the Lord in your hearts, giving thanks always and for everything in the name of our Lord Jesus Christ to God the Father"*—Eph 5:1-2; 19-20).

We look to Our Lady as the mirror to measure whether or not we are living this baptismal call as She did. Inevitably we will not live it perfectly—for She is the only Immaculate One—but all the more we must unite with Christ so that He can be our Savior. It is by accepting Christ's gift of laying down His life and washing His wife with His Word to make her perfect that we are given the grace we need to live His priesthood with Him. Ephesians 5:24-27 states:

> *"As the church is subordinate to Christ, so wives should be subordinate to their husbands in everything. Husbands, love your wives, even as Christ loved the church and handed himself over for her to sanctify her, cleansing her by the bath of water with the word, that he might present to himself the church in splendor, without spot or wrinkle or any such thing, that she might be holy and without blemish."*

In this we come to reflect Our Mother Mary in becoming completely one with Jesus, the Eternal High Priest. It is in virtue of this union that Jesus brings about with the Church collectively, as well as with each soul, that He draws us into His One priesthood to partake of it with Him each time we offer worship *"rejoicing always, praying without ceasing, and in all circumstances giving thanks, for this is the will of God for you in Christ Jesus"* (1 Thes 5:16-18). In this way, we offer sacrifice with Christ and thus can be a helpmate of those men drawn into His One Universal Priesthood. Our Lady did this perfectly first. We are called to imitate Her, as Her children, and do this as well.

Praying for Priests

Here at the end, we come to see clearly how souls are called by God to not only accept the priestly work of Christ in their own lives, but also to actively partake with Him in that saving work. All souls are called to this. And yet, there are special souls called by God to an even greater participation with Christ and His priests in their service of the Church. We are called to look at Mary in all of this—for She is the perfect model for us in all things. We are to pray with Christ (and His priest brothers) as She did; we are to serve Christ (and His priest brothers) just as She did; and we are called to love Christ (and His priest brothers) as She did—but living in union with Her Heart united always as one with Jesus.

Appendix

Chaplet of Sorrows for Priests

1 Our Father
1 Hail Mary
1 Creed

On each 'Our Father' bead of a rosary, say the Sorrow of Our Lady's Heart and a Hail Mary.
On each 'Hail Mary' bead of a rosary, say: *"O Sorrowful and Immaculate Heart of Mary, Pray for us who have recourse to Thee!"*

After all 7 decades, say 1 'Glory Be', 'Hail Holy Queen' and 'Memorare'

(You can also add the **'Stabat Mater'** if you would like.)

Seven Sorrows of Our Lady
(each one is a 'Mystery' of the Chaplet)

1. <u>First Sorrow</u> of Our Lady's Heart is the Prophesy of Simeon

2. <u>Second Sorrow</u> of Our Lady's Heart is the Flight into Egypt

3. <u>Third Sorrow</u> of Our Lady's Heart is the Losing of the Child Jesus in the Temple

4. <u>Fourth Sorrow</u> of Our Lady's Heart is when Mary Meets Jesus on His Way to Calvary

5. <u>Fifth Sorrow</u> of Our Lady's Heart is when Jesus Dies on the Cross

6. <u>Sixth Sorrow</u> of Our Lady's Heart is when Jesus is Taken Down from the Cross and Laid in Her Arms (the 'Pieta')

7. <u>Seventh Sorrow</u> of Our Lady's Heart is when Jesus is Taken from Her Arms and Laid in the Tomb

History of this Book

Over the last 25 years many people have known that my life was given in a special way to pray for priests and they have come to me asking advice as to how they could better live this ministry as well. And so for many years I have prayed about this question and answered people in various ways depending on what the Lord specifically gave to me for each one. In October, 2020, a woman approached me (who was recently asked to start a ministry at her parish to pray for their pastor) and asked me advice as to how to best pray for him (and priests in general). In answer to her question, the Lord gave me this book very quickly. I wrote the entire thing in a week or two, although the reflections have stirred in my heart for decades.

I pray that this book is a great blessing to all women (and men) called to offer their lives in praying for priests. I also pray that all priests who read it are touched by the examples of Jesus, Mary and the saints herein. I pray that their hearts become more con-formed to Christ because of these reflections. I pray that their lives become more dependent on Our Lady, according to Jesus' example in His Priesthood. And I pray that the examples of the saints inspire them to reach the holiness God destined for each one of them in their own priestly vocations.

For more information about Mary Kloska's vocation, books, icons (Artist Shop), music, podcasts or to become a monthly donor to support her ministry, please see:
www.marykloskafiat.com
Blog: http://fiatlove.blogspot.com
Donations: https://www.patreon.com/marykloskafiat

Books

The Holiness of Womanhood

https://enroutebooksandmedia.com/holinessofwomanhood

Out of the Darkness

https://enroutebooksandmedia.com/outofthedarkness

Radio

Podcasts: https://wcatradio.com/heartoffiatcrucifiedlove

YouTube VIDEO Podcasts

Playlist: http://www.tinyurl.com/marykloska

Artist Shop (Icon prints and other items for sale): http://marykloskafiat.threadless.com

Music CD "FIAT" available on all music platforms.

Facebook: https://www.facebook.com/mary.kloska.7

Appendix

Some Praise for *In Our Lady's Shadow*

"Mary Kloska's book *In Our Lady's Shadow – The Spirituality of Praying for Priests* is one of the most motivational contemporary Catholic books I have ever read. In our time of crisis in the Church, it is of vital importance that we be praying for priests in a way even more intense than before. Read it! It may enrich your own spiritual life in a way you cannot predict." – Ronda Chervin, Ph.D., retired Catholic Philosophy Professor, author of numerous books, and presenter on EWTN and Catholic Radio

"Published on International Women's Day, Mary Kloska's new book... *IN OUR LADY'S SHADOW: The Spirituality of Praying for Priests...* is a timely reflection on the beautiful mission that women in particular have of praying for priests. At a time when many women find themselves confused regarding their role in society and their place in the Church... the Body of Christ... the author points out the special, maternal giftedness of womanhood and the wonderful spirituality that flows from this reality. The author reminds women that, contrary to popular opinion, it is "littleness" that makes the biggest difference in this world." – **Fr. Lawrence Edward Tucker, SOLT... author of** *The Prayer of Jesus Crucified*, *Adventures in the Father's Joy!*, *To Whom the Heart Decided to Love*, *The Redemption of San Isidro.*

"This book is a wonderful resource for young men studying for the priesthood, a beloved parish priest or priest friend, as well as anyone who feels drawn to pray for priests. It is a treasure trove of insight and gold mine of inspiration, so needed in this challenging modern world." – Theresa Thomas, Family Columnist, Mother of nine, and author of *Big Hearted* (**Scepter**)

"As a mother of small children and someone dedicated to praying weekly holy hours for priests, this book helps me to love more deeply the devotions of priests and how much they need our prayers. I am so pleased to have it as a guide. A very special book!" – Amelia Colone, wife, mother and member of the Seven Sisters Apostolate of weekly adoration for priests

For more, please visit Mary Kloska on En Route Books and Media at https://enroutebooksandmedia.com/shadow/

Made in the USA
Monee, IL
13 April 2023

31568485R00089